THE SWEDISH MEATBALL BIBLE

Hungry for more inspiration? Dig in at:
www.kottbullsbloggen.se

BULLET POINT PUBLISHING

www.bulletpointpublishing.se

© Claes Grahn Moller, Ralph Lindgren, Hans-Olov Öberg, 2014

English Translation: Swedish Word Mafia, Los Angeles, California

Design: Sanna Sporrong Form (sannasporrongform.se)

Photographer: Nina Schwab and Sofia Ejheden

Cover: Niklas Lindblad, Mystical Garden Design

Photographer wrap: Nina Schwab

Press: GPS Group / Ednas print, Slovenia, 2015

ISBN: 978-91-88153-05-0

Claes Grahn-Möller   Ralph Lindgren   Hans-Olov Öberg

THE
SWEDISH MEATBALL BIBLE

BULLET POINT PUBLISHING

TABLE OF CONTENTS

WHO WRITES A MEATBALL BIBLE, ANYWAY?

CLAES GRAHN-MÖLLER had a distinctive appetite as a child. This made Grandma Anna from Edsbyn understandably worried, but she knew what it took to please him. She served special meatballs with lots of cream in a smooth, light and very creamy sauce with mashed potatoes that were also smothered in cream. Little did grandmother Anna know that with this she would completely shape her grandson's relationship to meatballs – which would, in turn, end up launching him into a star-studded chef's career.

And so, Claes couldn't help himself from striving to refine and perfect any meatball served at the restaurants he oversaw. At the longstanding Restaurant Diana, he had to take a step back from the excesses surrounding the meatball served there and dial it back to a rendition of the classic Swedish meatball, complete with all the accessories this jewel-of-a-food requires.

In Paris – where Claes occupied, among other positions, head chef at the Swedish embassy and worked with star chef Alain Passard of L'Arpege restaurant – there was plenty of room to improve and refine, often using veal and all other types of mixtures of ground meat – and always using cream as a flavor carrier.

Sometimes, the assignment required a certain level of mass production – for example, during Christmas time, when maintaining a high level of quality brought particular challenges.

Something that would affect this book's story (and perhaps even, eventually, the reader's meatball life) occurred when Claes was 17 years old: he became allergic to fish and shellfish. The young Grahn-Moller – his career in restaurants already well underway – experienced his fair share of jealousy over anyone who ate pickled herring during the holidays.

But many years later, during the dinner that was a catalyst for beginning work on this book, an idea came to light: what about a *pickled* meatball? This would function as a complement to herring dishes served during the holidays. Immediately, Claes went home and created a recipe that struck all the taste testers with amazement and love. Perhaps in the future, "The Swedish Pickled Meatball" will accompany "The Classic Swedish Meatball" on the dining table?

Today, Claes spends his time working in quality control for one of Sweden's largest grocery chains. He also coaches children and young teens in sports.

Growing up in the culinary desert of the '60s and '70s, **RALPH LINDGREN'S** diet during childhood and adolescence consisted largely of canned ravioli, sour milk and Eterna with powdered sugar, chili con carne, meatballs and macaroni; and on festive occasions, beef tenderloin drenched in mushroom sauce and then baked in a puff pastry. His sense of taste was broadened thanks to nannies from Finland who offered up Karelian pierogies and even *memmas* – traditional

Finnish Easter treats – served with sour cream. A pattern appeared time and time again in the home as a result of certain eating habits and food from Lebanon, Japan, Mexico and other exotic places. As a result, in 1974 Ralph could eat his meatballs and macaroni with chopsticks.

His mother's recipe for meatballs came from the Big Cookbook. It was an excellent, classic meatball recipe. Meatballs were made with great care, but without fail, some would exit her cast iron pan with flat bottoms. Even today, Ralph's over-80-year-old mother makes good meatballs every week (with flat bottoms found here and there). In the Big Cookbook, instructions were given regarding everything that concerned food and drink. Even as a 12-year-old, Ralph studied topics like which glass was suitable for an "after dinner cocktail," and how to quickly butcher a lamb. During his university years, Ralph's interest in meatballs grew at the same rate as the cash in his wallet disappeared. In 1994, he attended the "Renstierna Meatball Open," discovering that there were more people fascinated by the meatball than he ever imagined – and with this his meatball interest reached new heights. Before holidays, Ralph engaged in intensive dialogue with other passionate meatball fans about new ways to further refine and multiply meatballs, with the hopes of their ending up on various holiday buffet tables. Now and then, Ralph goes into the forest to hunt, allowing him to produce various meatballs made of meat and meat mixtures from Swedish game. Ralph is the proud owner of a hand-cranked meat grinder. His mother has a similar one.

HANS-OLOV ÖBERG'S love of meatballs began early. It was his father Olle who cooked the family meatballs, following a recipe passed down from previous generations; thus the myth of "Momma's Meatballs" never got passed down in the Öberg family. The meatballs were small and based on three types of ground meat in a recipe somewhat reminiscent of what was presented in the Princesses' Cookbook, a popular cookbook for earlier generations.

His love for meatballs was engrained during adolescence with young Hans-Olov eventually taking over the family's traditional recipe. But it was the idea of a meatball contest between teams of good friends that launched his career in meatballs. After having arranged the "Renstierna Meatball Open" along with a bunch of friends (in which they could compete in "Classic" and "Custom" categories), Hans-Olov had finally gotten a real taste for it all.

The meatballs from Grandma Hilda's recipe are on the Christmas table – a distinguished and highly regarded dish. Both of the Öberg family's kids help with rolling and frying the batter.

Standing outside the kitchen is Hans-Olov: publisher, writer and financial strategy adviser. He is a passionate fan of his local Swedish soccer team, and spends substantial amounts of time with a variety of musical instruments as well as the family's puppy (which will eventually get meatball nutrition reinforcement when he grows up).

INTRODUCTION

WELCOME TO THIS ORGY FOR MEATBALL ENT-HUSIASTS! Meatballs have seen a resurgence in re-cent times and are now available as standard dishes in most restaurants. In Stockholm, Sweden, there is even a boutique completely specialized in meatballs. And as we travel more and more, we can see an increase in the variety of meatballs found throughout the world.

In some places, you can see different species at the same time. It may involve mass-produced meatballs at a lower price-per-kilo than sawdust, coming from a dubious source and with unknown ingredients. But it may also encompass gourmet restaurants serving pickled meatballs instead of pressed, and having the nerve to label meatballs with a 6-7 cm diameter as "Classic Swedish Meatballs." No offense to these meatballs, but "Classic Swedish" they are not.

What is the meatball world we will leave to our children? We want this juicy and inspirational book simply to inspire greater experimentation with meatballs so that they will live on for many centuries to come. Hopefully, the children born all around the world today will continue to enjoy both classic Swe-dish meatballs (we have an abundant section about this in the book, where all ingredients are described in detail) and also innovative new ones (of which there are many between these pages).

A HISTORY OF MEATBALLS

SWEDISH MEATBALLS ACCOMPANIED Swedish emigrants to the USA, just as other versions accompanied immigrants from other countries such as Italy.

The fact that the meatball is now a worldwide dish is a testament to humanity. The meatball has many appealing features. When money is tight, bread, spices, vegetables and other things can be added to the meat. Hammered meat is also the method used for those who want to store the meat for longer periods and then use it later. Meatballs can be endlessly customized, adapted to local customs, and used in different, creative ways. In the next chapter, we'll take a look at the popularity of the meatball in today's global cuisine.

It is easy to imagine how the meatball's popularity spread through all the channels of the Roman Empire. In fact, the history of its expansion and impact is reminiscent of how the Swedish meatball is today spread via IKEA.

But let's change continents for a moment. Even in ancient China, early meatball-like dishes arose. Emperor Yang, who was part of the Sui Dynasty (581-619 AD), gave a mandate to his chefs to create dishes that celebrated a number of beautiful places he visited during his travels in Yangzhou province. And to honor Kuihua Gang (translated as sunflower ridge), a dish was created with large meatballs served in lettuce leaves. Initially, the dish was titled sunflower meat, but a hundred years later, the Emperor gave it its current name – lion heads – because the undeniably delicious meatballs are said to recall that same taste. And in the right light and the right conditions, one can imagine it just might.

Another story of innovation from China – this time taking place about 1600 AD – concerns a man named Meng Bo, who realized that his old mother could no longer eat meat because she was not able to chew it.

The young Chinaman – renowned for his maternal love and general good morals – ended up inventing the gung wang, which are cooked pork-based meatballs.

The mother was afforded the renewed opportunity to eat meat again and meatballs became a smash hit in the neighborhood around Fuzhou. Good recipes for both lion heads and gung wang are easy to find on the Internet, and are for that reason not listed in this book.

Looking again to the West, the Roman Empire spread meatballs to many countries around Europe and, not least, the Arab countries. There, the dish was based on lamb and was named kofte – probably after the Persian word koffteh, meaning hammered meat.

During the Arab conquest of Spain, meatballs spread back across the Mediterranean in the form of albondigas (the name derives from the Arabic al-bunduq, which literally means hazelnut, but also can be interpreted as a description of a small, round object).

The British, who might not be primarily known for their meatballs, were equally quick to begin serving our favorite dish. As early as the 1400s, there were meatballs in the recipe collection *Potage Dyvers* – potentially published the very same year that Joan of Arc was burned at the stake – in which meatballs were presented using the name pompers.

Was it the warrior king Karl XII who brought meatballs to Sweden from his conquests in Turkey? Many argue that it came at the same time stuffed cabbage arrived in Sweden. No matter how it happened, meatballs can be found in Cajsa Warg's cookbook from 1755, *The Young Woman's Little Household Helper*.

MEATBALLS IN THE WORLD

MEATBALLS ARE GLOBAL. There seems to be something fundamental about using meat – of good quality, or simply that which happens to be at hand – and flavoring it quickly, rolling it into round balls, cooking and serving it. There are countries where the meatball was elevated from a commonplace dish to a fancy one – in Tanzania, for example – but in general the meatball is a simple, delicious and sensible food for ordinary people. People like you and me. However, there are spots on the map where the traditional kitchen chef can't help but constantly flatten the meat mixture into patties or similar shapes. Austria is one such example where this traditional staple food has never had, nor ever will have (according to the Austrians themselves) a place at the table. Meat is not commonplace in all countries and cultures, either. Some cultures simply don't have or use a lot of meat in their cuisine; or, they have other traditions, and other ingredients are used to provide the protein content of meals, such as soy-based foods common to Asia.

In a global perspective, meatballs are primarily a commoner's dish. Of course you can find meatballs at fine restaurants around the world, flavored with the country's own special spices, sauces and accessories.

But there are exceptions to this too. One explanation may be that the fine dining restaurant guests in many countries lack confidence in what the restaurants' chefs put in their meat batter.

Sweden and the southeastern parts of Africa, perhaps primarily Zanzibar, probably have the world's smallest meatballs, measuring only 2-3 cm in diameter. Most other countries' meatballs are so large that 2-3 pieces are enough for an entire meal. Some unorthodox pubs in Sweden have taken this to heart and – even though they know it's wrong – serve what they claim are "classic Swedish meatballs," despite having a diameter of 6-7 centimeters.

If you hang in Forodhani on Zanzibar on a Friday night you can order a "mix" from one of the street stalls. In it you'll find deep-fried mini meatballs (beef, 2 cm in maximum diameter) mixed with diced, stewed potatoes and flavored with turmeric, chili and fried cassava. The street food chef Mzee Adnani is said to have invented the dish that has become hugely popular and is now also served at swank hotels in Tanzania. However, Tanzanian meatballs from the home kitchen, known as *kebabo*, are usually much larger, often as big as Swedish meatballs. They are flavored with whatever

spices the chef can find in the cupboard and then deep-fried. In Swahili, meatballs are likewise called *kebabo*. Both the word and the dish were brought to Africa in the late 1000s A.D. via the Persians.

In Tunisia, meatballs are called *Kaaber* and are a traditional dish available in all sizes, meat types, and seasonings. Cumin and mint are popular and meatballs are flavorful but almost never spicy. Cauliflower as an ingredient in the meatball is a crowd favorite. Unfortunately, the future of meatballs in Tunisia is uncertain. Traditional food is generally in decline, with few being taught momma's old recipes (apologies for the gender generalization). Many would rather fancy themselves as modern eaters, employing recipes from Western countries. In Morocco and Lebanon, meatballs are better rooted in the soul of the people, but even so, you can't find meatballs on the menu at fine dining restaurants. In most Muslim countries, meatballs are very rarely served as a stand-alone dish. However, it is common to see them as one of many dishes on the buffet table at Ramadan.

In the Australian film *Sunday Too Far Away*, there is a scene where hardened, tired-out sheep shearers sit and watch the camp's chef molding the evening's dinner meatballs in his hairy, sweaty armpit. A lesson in outback culture can be drawn from this: Australian meatballs are seemingly about as big as a chef's armpit and obviously prepared BBQ-style. The film has received a great number of awards and is highly recommended.

Once the grill is lit, Australians like to make meatballs like rissoles – adding eggs, salt and pepper, breadcrumbs, onion, and often grated carrot.

Although meatballs in the country of Georgia do not really count as traditional food, they are a common ingredient in soups found there. The meatballs are cooked – usually in water, tomato paste and onions – and served immediately, sometimes with a dollop of sour cream. In Sweden, breadcrumbs are often used to allow moisture to remain in the meatball. In Georgia, Ukraine and neighboring countries, rice is used to accomplish this. Ukrainian meatballs (at 3-8 cm in diameter) are a traditional food made with ground pork. They are fried and served with a choice of sauce, usually tomato-based.

Romanians are convinced that the Swedish meatball is actually Romanian. When the Swedish army was beaten at Poltava in 1709 and Charles XII conceded defeat, a thousand Swedes and several thousand Cossacks marched towards the Ottoman Empire. Their first stop was Tighina in Moldova (known as *Bender* in Turkish). Between 1711 and 1713, King Charles and his entourage lived just outside the village Varnitsa. It is likely that the Swedes enjoyed Romanian meatballs so much that they brought them home to Sweden. In Romania, the meatball is called a *chiftele* (from the Turkish word *kofte*), and in Moldova it is called a *parjoale* and is clearly larger than the Romanian variety. The entire region loves their meatballs, preparing them in any number of ways (although frying is the most common), serving them in all types of combinations, and spicing them with whatever tastes right. Apparently, in this region, only imagination limits how ground meat is used. Could this area of the world be meatball heaven?

The size of ping pong balls, made with a mixture of half beef and half pork, and on the menu at least once a month in every household, school cafeteria and lunch restaurant, Slovenian meatballs are served with mashed potatoes and a tomato-based sauce. This can seem like it is a mixture of Italian and Romanian recipes, and is the most common way to serve meatballs in the country. The only major difference is that Slovenians generally boil their meatballs.

Young children in Canada are brought up well. As kids, they learn a meatball song. At home, in kindergarten, in school and at camp, the "Meatball Chant" is with them everywhere. And if you ask a Canadian to dig deep into their memory of the meatball chant, chances are high that they'll begin to sing it right then and there. The Canadian meatball recipe is imported from Italy. Spaghetti and meatballs in a spaghetti sauce is a favorite. In recent years, the Swedish smorgasbord has started to become fashionable, and with it Swedish Meatballs (even though Swedes would probably not recognize them).

The USA is a diverse culture, and a place where all the world's meatballs are represented – even if the Italian meatball dominates. If you stumble into a Ukrainian restaurant in the Bronx, it's not impossible to find large meatballs made of ground pork and served with a tomato-based sauce. Meatballs are hard to find in traditional American cuisine. It is worth noting that the Swedish cultural imperialism brought on by IKEA has put Swedish meatballs on many an Americans' agenda. Maybe this is Sweden's subtle payback for McDonald's and Coca-Cola.

Most Swedes have at some time been to Spain and eaten *albondigas*, a classic of Spanish cuisine. Much like people talk about their mother's or grandmother's meatballs, Spaniards talk about their *albondigas*: "Good, yes, but not like grandmother's." The dish is served as tapas, often with a tomato-based sauce. Neighboring Portugal doesn't have the same strong connection to their *almôndegas*; they are traditional but not very popular. Rare for a European country, Portugal never serves their meatballs with sauce, though they rarely add sauce to any of their cuisine.

Lion heads is a globally diversified Chinese meatball dish, but historically China has not had a particularly high consumption of meat, opting instead for soy-based raw ingredients that make up a large part of Chinese protein intake. And as soon as you wrap your meatball in rice paper or anything else, it ceases to be a meatball, and turns into a dumpling – or ravioli, depending on where you are in the world.

Throw some mint, coriander, chili, lime juice and *nuoc mam* (fish sauce) in the batter, and your meatballs will end up tasting like they are from Vietnam.

Asia is simple like that: they use ground beef spiked with what suits the region's taste buds. This works for places like India, Pakistan, Cambodia, Laos, Korea, Thailand and many others.

Mix and match with cardamom, star anise, cloves, cinnamon, nutmeg, ginger, turmeric, galangal, garlic, shallots, lemongrass, coriander and lime. If you're looking for more of a Cambodian flavor, you obviously have to season with *prahok*, or fermented fish paste, which is an important basic ingredient in the country's cuisine. In general, however, meat is eaten quite infrequently in Cambodia. Which types of meat are eaten in which Asian countries is usually something the local religion governs.

And just like China, France – the food country par excellence – has numerous different regions with their own culinary traditions. Many regions have meatballs in their traditional cuisine, others don't. When you think of French food, you might think of "the new French cuisine", with a couple of artfully arranged peas and a tsp of sauce, where meatballs are as unthinkable on the plate as lederhosen are on the chef. This is not so in reality. "Rustic," "lush" and "saucy" are terms that fit very well with traditional meatballs in France. What is a bit odd is that Frenchmen happily infuse their meatballs in other dishes such as potato au gratin with baked meatballs, cold potato salad with pieces of meatball, ratatouille with meatballs, Julienne soup with meatballs, and more. Flip through French recipe books and food websites and you'll often find *boulettes de viande sauce suédoise*, which, as one might guess, are *Swedish meatballs with cream sauce*. But you will not find pickled cucumber and lingonberries as sides. However, the French are of course world champions when it comes to mashed potatoes. Get your hands on a bag of potatoes (type 'BF 15') and follow the recipe on page 42: you'll soon find yourself among the mashed potato world elite.

In 1975, the Brazilian rock band The Meatballs (*Almôndegas*) released their eponymous LP entitled The Meatballs (*Almôndegas*). Neither the tape nor LP made any great impact on music history, but the band name alludes to a meatball culture, at least in the southeastern regions of Brazil. There, it is common to add the meatballs in a broth-like soup with vegetables or whatever. Many Brazilians think it's a traditional winter food. They come home, into the warmth, and make *calditos* with vegetables, adding the newly fried meatballs or allowing them cook themselves in the hot soup, making for a nice hot meal on a cold day.

Argentina is meat heaven for many. The environmental impact of the giant herds of cattle grazing on the great plains is most probably discussed less in Argentina than in, for example, a country like Sweden. Regardless, meatballs are likewise a tradition in the whole of the country. Meatball recipes pass from generation to generation, and have done so for hundreds of years. History assumes that meatballs in Argentina come from Persia, via Spain through the centuries of Muslim presence there. Of course, Argentines make their own variations of meatballs using different flavorings and mixing herbs and spices in the meat batter, then frying, deep-frying or boiling them. But there is still a popular, basic recipe that includes ground beef, egg, milk, and breadcrumbs.

Perhaps we recognize these ingredients from somewhere? The traditional Argentine meatball sauce consists of shallots fried in olive oil, broth, flour, white wine, salt and pepper.

In Central America, ground beef is an important ingredient in cooking. But chicken is the predominant raw ingredient used for protein. And this is true for the whole of the Caribbean archipelago. A specialty for Central America is crocodile meatballs (or alligator meatballs as we call them in the recipe. The name alligator probably comes from the Spanish *el Lagarto*, meaning lizard). The American crocodile (*Crocodylus acutus*), is spread throughout Central America from southern Florida and the Caribbean in the east to the north of Mexico and from there to the south of Peru and Venezuela. Crocodiles can grow large, to over 4-5 meters long, and can be dangerous to humans. But they are surprisingly good to eat as meatballs!

Do not confuse Mexican cuisine with tex mex cooking. The word is a blend of *Texan* from Texas, and *Mexican*, and makes up a cuisine that is popular in the southern United States. When Mexicans eat meatballs, they do so almost always in a soup, often tomato-based.

Russia, like Austria, has difficulties holding back the urge to flatten their meatballs into something more like ground beef patties. Therefore, it's quite unusual to meet a Russian who wants to treat you to meatballs (*frikadelka*). And when they do, you can bet your last Ruble they are more or less flat. In the odd chance they do appear spherical, it is often in a soup. Moreover, Russia is a huge country and has many different culinary traditions; as such, there are almost certainly meatball deserts here – regions without meatballs but with plenty of ground beef patties.

In the past it was considered almost disrespectful to ask the butcher for ground beef, because it could be interpreted to mean that one could not afford to buy real meat but only ground up spare parts.

Japan is a developed country when it comes to meatballs – which might be pointing out the obvious. Here, the raw ingredient's original form is generally secure. In recent decades, the Japanese have woken up to, and gotten more and more interested in, other countries' cooking. Swedes, Moroccans, Spaniards, Italians and other expats are hired to hold cooking courses in the homes of interested Japanese. Just like in the USA, IKEA has helped to spread the meatball gospel in Japan.

A CLASSIC MEATBALL

TO BEGIN, WE WANT TO GIVE A GOOD PIECE OF ADVICE.
Make sure the ingredients are the same temperature when the preparation starts. At different temperatures, the ingredients cooperate in different ways and are not nearly as good together. They mix less naturally and the flavor-carrying fat is not retained as well in the meatballs. Ready? Here we go!

THE GROUND MEAT
The ground meat is the starting point. Without really good ground meat, meatballs are simply not as good. And what is it that makes good ground meat? The quality of meat is the starting point. The meat should always be fresh and freshly ground. Certainly, there is factory-ground meat that survives up to eight days in the fridge, but everything has a price and in this case the price is stringiness in texture and taste. We therefore recommend that you either grind the meat yourself – certainly a premium option (but if you have time, it becomes both the nicest and best way to get the ground meat you desire) – or look at getting retail-ground or slaughterhouse-ground meat (a rarity).

More recently, collagen has been frequently discussed regarding ground meat. Collagen is located closest to the legs of the animal – the connective tissue, tendons and the like – and therefore we do not want it in our ground meat. If you buy meat and get it ground, or grind it yourself, you avoid this problem elegantly.

And what meat are we talking about? Primarily Chuck. Beef should make up about seventy percent of the total. The reason behind our choice of chuck is that it is the optimum composition of meat and fat. The fat content is about fifteen percent, and it should stay thereabouts in order for the meatballs to taste really good.

Meat cubes for stew are often made from prime rib or brisket. If they are brisket-based, which contain very little fat, you should choose a fattier ground pork to combine it with. Another type of fat, oil or butter can never replace animal fat in the ground meat.

We use pork for the second part of the ground meat blend. And not just any pork, but preferably some form of free-range farmed pork. And if you can, choose the loin, for precisely the same reasons as the prime rib – it has a good ratio of fat. Using average retail pork as a raw ingredient is nothing to be asha-

med of, but it's usually made up of several different elements: shoulder, loin, side, roast pork, scraps and, well, everything else.

How coarsely should the beef be ground?

Grinding to a size of 2-4 mm is most appropriate. At retail, ground beef is generally midway between coarsely- and finely-ground. For example, when making a traditionally Swedish Wallenbergare (a highly recommended dish, go Google it), the aim is to have veal ground as finely as possible – preferably ground twice, to "smash" together the tendons and fibers in the meat and create something more akin to puree than ground beef. That's not how we make Swedish meatballs!

For honest, old-fashioned meatballs, we do not want the finest grind: that's better suited for upscale, smaller sandwich-type meatballs, or perhaps Mediterranean-inspired meatballs (We will return to this subject in greater detail later in the book).

But meatballs are also about having luck while making them. If you aren't able to get your hands on an optimal meat blend as described above, just try to make the best of the situation, as an important part of the end result depends on the love of the dish.

BREADCRUMBS

What function do soaked breadcrumbs really fill? It's about two things: juiciness and fat-binding.

The goal when frying the meatball properly is to get the fat to remain in the meatball. Therefore, we use breadcrumbs as a way to bind fat. The opposite – when the fat leaves the meatball – results in small, hard balls that please no one.

There are many different varieties of bread that can be used in the meatball. But the choice of which bread is not vital, so use what you feel is best.

White bread is most traditionally used in loaf form (everything works if you cut off the edges). It is soaked – preferably the day before but at least one hour before use. During soaking, a milk with the highest fat content should be used. At the very least, use whole milk. These are real meatballs we're making, not some sort of diet food.

ONION

The onion should be yellow. Big, small, old or fresh – it doesn't matter. But dicing it is important. This is the truly geeky practice of diligently chopping the onion so the result is an onion diced into millimeter-sized pieces only after two movements of the knife – once per direction. Hold onto the root of the onion when you dice it – that way the onion stays together better. Dicing in a crisscross fashion squeezes out the bitter flavors, which then become more potent in the batter. This also happens when the onion is torn apart by hand, or a machine is used to chop it.

A clever middle path for those who are not really drawn to onion dicing is to chop the onion roughly at first, then sauté and cook it in butter until its surface is lightly browned. And then run it through the blender.

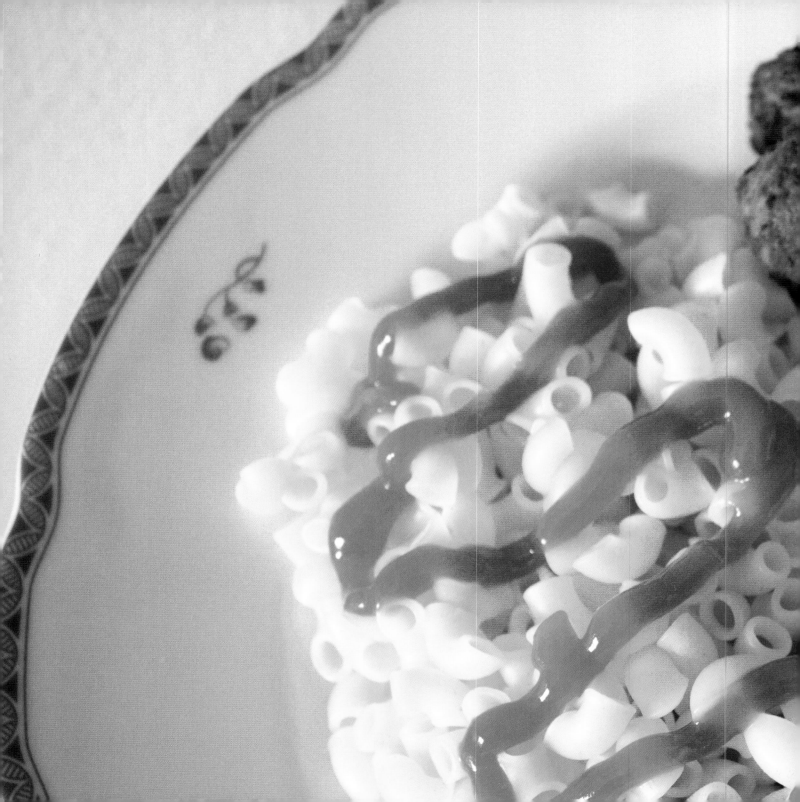

This avoids breaking the bulb, which creates a bitter taste when it evaporates.

SEASONING

In the best of worlds, just two spices are required for the optimal, classic meatball: salt (ordinary table salt is excellent), and freshly ground white pepper. End of story.

How much it is seasoned, however, is of utmost importance. To use the oft-cited rule of "one milliliter of salt per kilogram of ground beef" is borderline frivolous in our eyes. We think the best way to do things is to test-fry a seasoned meatball, eat it, spice it up a little more, and repeat until the balance is just right.

EGGS

What use does egg have in the batter? Again, it has to do with binding fat and maintaining the structure of the meatball. And what is important in this context? Not to overdose on eggs. Both eggs and ground beef contain similar types of binders, and overuse of either or both will result in firm or downright hard meatballs. Loose grind can sometimes get swept up in excessive egg remaining after the majority of it is already in the batter. But consider for a minute how a boiled egg looks. Is that how you want your meatballs to look?

PROCESSING THE BATTER

Use your (meticulously cleaned) hand as a dough hook. Only you can tell how the batter is feeling. Additionally, a household blender with dough hooks on a low speed setting can work too. An old-fashioned kitchen assistant with a good head on their shoulders works equally well.

The goal is to mix together all the ingredients until they feel like a cohesive batter. Use common sense and your sense of feel to avoid overprocessing the batter. Otherwise you risk making the meatballs stringy.

ROLLING

There are almost as many variations of rolling as there are aspiring meatball chefs. For meals serving up to four people it is always best to roll the balls by hand, with slightly damp hands.

Use personal taste to determine size. Avoid really small and really big meatballs. The small ones used in sandwiches dry out too easily and are boring, and the large cannonball-sized ones that are all-too-often served at large restaurants usually require additional preparation. It's difficult to get a uniformly fine texture all the way through large balls, and less scrupulous cooks often take shortcuts by boiling them in sauce or roasting them in the oven after frying (which results in a flat-bottomed ball – something perceived as lackluster and mass-produced).

A good rule of thumb for determining meatball size is rolling a ball that you can split once with a fork and then comfortably eat.

Spoon rolling is another option. Those who have a propensity to use spoons do not have to stop. Piping the meatball batter is something especially large restaurants engage in. Do not do this at home. Piping is about gaining time: the poor meatballs don't come out quite round enough, and the old chef's joke about rolling balls with your armpit providing that "extra kick" to the seasoning may be better off staying an old wives' tale?

FRYING

In the classic image of a frying pan full of meatballs, a traditional cast iron pan is always used. But with modern technological developments, there are now plenty of alternative options. The bottom needs to be thick, regardless of the choice of pan, so that the heat is distributed evenly across all the balls.

The oil blend may be a mixture of rapeseed oil and butter. A blend like this doesn't go too dark, allowing for longer and warmer frying than butter does. But when it comes to flavor profile, butter has an understandable desirability.

First pour in the oil and heat for a bit. Then add butter. When the butter is silent, it's time to add in the first meatballs. The goal – and this cannot be stressed enough – is to fry the meatballs, not to boil them in their own juice. Therefore, it can be helpful to limit the number of meatballs per round of frying.

Make sure to keep the balls moving! Speed should be sufficiently high so that the balls will not rest and flatten on one side. A pan with sloping sides helps facilitate this.

Fry the meatballs until they are ready. Don't overcook them. If you're wondering if they are cooked just right, any uncertainty can be mitigated by simply sacrificing a meatball or two, but don't take more than that. Expect that they'll cook a little extra after being placed in the serving bowl.

ACCESSORIES

MASHED POTATOES

FOR THOSE WHO WANT TO SERVE A GENUINE SWEDISH MEATBALL MEAL
THERE ARE NO SHORTCUTS. ONE MUST MAKE HOMEMADE MASHED POTA-
TOES. UNDERSTANDABLY, THEY ARE BEST WHEN THEY TURN OUT REALLY
VELVETY AND SOFT. BUT HOW DO WE ACHIEVE THIS?
BEGIN ONE HOUR BEFORE THE FOOD IS SERVED.

USE:

1 kg potatoes – select potatoes of uniform size, so
that they cook with the same consistency . . . .
2-3 dl whole milk . . . .
250 g cold butter . . . .
Sea salt (10 g per liter of water). . . . .

DIRECTIONS:

Naturally the potatoes are the main ingredient.
And although in an emergency virtually any spud
will do, BF 15 potatoes provide the absolute best
results. It is an oblong potato variety grown in
France and coveted by virtuoso chefs like Joël
Robuchon. The beauty of the BF 15 – which can be
replaced by Dutch Timate or German Nicola in a
pinch – is firmness. It is simply the optimal potato
for holding together the mash and providing it with
the proper airy, smooth texture.

Make sure to wash the potatoes well and boil
them with the skin on. Do not let them cool in the
cooking water. If they do, they will taste like they've
been reheated.

Peel the potatoes while they are still hot and cut
them into slices. Then mash the potatoes as fine as
possible (using a potato masher, as a blender will
make the mash sticky and elastic) and deposit into
a heavy-bottomed saucepan. Put the pan on low
heat and stir vigorously with a wooden spoon for 4-5
minutes.

Slice the butter – which should be very cold – into
small cubes. Stir in three-quarters of the butter,
piece by piece, until it is absorbed into the mash.

Add three-quarters of (very) hot milk, stirring
gently and continuously.

Continue to stir until all the liquid is absorbed
and the mash feels really smooth. If it feels heavy
and sticky, add more butter and milk while stirring
vigorously. Using a normal, hand-held kitchen whisk,
whisk the mash into an airy consistency.

Now let's add the finishing touches: squeeze the
mash through a sieve (using a flat, fine-meshed
sieve) to get it as fine as possible.

Then keep the mash warm by placing the pan in
warm water until it is ready to be served. Stir oc-
casionally so that the mash stays soft.

And finally, present the mashed potatoes in a pleasant way: in a bowl, by piping them on the serving
plate, or in another nice fashion.

CUCUMBER

ONE CAN SOMETIMES RUN INTO UNCONSCIONABLE PICKLE CHOICES BY WAY OF CHEFS WHO REGULARLY INSULT THEIR GUESTS BY SERVING LENGTH-CUT PICKLES WITH MEATBALLS! FRESH CUCUMBER, CUCUMBERS SLICED TOO THICK, AND CUCUMBERS THAT HAVE NOT BEEN PRESSED (AS DESCRIBED BELOW) LEFT TO THEIR FATE IN THE LUNCH RUSH ARE OTHER ABOMINATIONS. HOW DO YOU GET TO THAT PERFECT SWEET-SOUR TASTE? THE STARTING POINT IS SWEDISH CUCUMBERS. TO PEEL OR NOT TO PEEL? THOSE WHO WISH MAY NATURALLY PEEL THEM, BUT WE RECOMMEND SERVING THE CUCUMBER UNPEELED. SLICE THE CUCUMBER THIN.

MAKE A PICKLE SOLUTION WITH THE FOLLOWING PROPORTIONS PER CUCUMBER:

3 tbsp vinegar – Winborgs 12-percent vinegar

6 tbsp granulated sugar . . . .

3 tbsp water . . . .

Chopped parsley . . . .

DIRECTIONS:

Place everything in a bowl with the sliced cucumber.

Place a plate on top of the cucumber mixture and put something heavy on top of the plate so that the cucumber is pressed down really hard.

Let it sit for about a day. The cucumber is perfectly ready to be eaten at once, but it will be even better if it can sit for longer.

═══ LINGONBERRY ═══

LINGONBERRY SAUCE IS EASY TO PREPARE; MOST FINE DINING
RESTAURANTS USUALLY SUCCEED VERY WELL WITH IT. BUT OF
COURSE THERE ARE PITFALLS. NO MEATBALL-MAKER WITH ANY
SELF-ESTEEM SERVES ANYTHING PRE-BOUGHT OR CANNED.

USE:

1 package frozen lingonberries . . . .

Equal parts sugar . . . .

FOR BEST RESULTS:

Take the package of frozen berries, an equal
amount of sugar, and mix together. When the berries have thawed and the sugar has melted, it is
ready.

An exciting variation that produces a delightful
result comes from mixing the frozen lingonberries
with Coca-Cola. 0.5 dl of cola is enough for 400 g
of lingonberries, and the taste is surprisingly good.

SAUCE

THE SAUCE PERFORMS MANY FUNCTIONS. IT WILL BE
STYLISH IN COLOR, TASTY AND HAVE A NATURAL TEXTURE.
THE WORST THAT CAN HAPPEN IS WHEN GOOD MEATBALLS
ARE SERVED WITH A TASTELESS SAUCE OR A SAUCE WITH
THE CONSISTENCY OF POWDER.

USE:

1 dl veal stock – we recommend Bong's Touch of
Taste . . . .
1 tsp currant jelly, either black or red . . . .
5 dl cream . . . .

DIRECTIONS:

Boil down until the consistency feels good.
Season with salt and pepper.

BASIC RECIPES

THE THREE BASIC RECIPES FOR MEATBALLS

WHY THREE BASIC RECIPES FOR MEATBALLS VARIATIONS?

• Variations of our beloved meatballs can go on indefinitely. But common features can be found in the foundation of all meatballs. And to simplify for the home chef, we have chosen to break down the more exotic varieties of meatball into three families:

• The Mediterranean Family – consists of common features found in kofte, albondigas, petites boulettes de viande, Italian meatballs, and so on. This requires a finer grind that gives strength to larger-size balls, while the balls are at the same time seasoned with various extra ingredients – cheese, fresh herbs, olives and the like – otherwise, these big meatballs can be really boring to eat.

• The Asian Family – consists of pork or poultry, "use what you have at hand"-meatballs that can pop up just about anywhere on trips to Asia's southeastern parts. These ball types can include cooked rice and more, and are usually a bit smaller in size. Not infrequently, they show up in soups, woks and other local dishes.

• The Beef Family – not so reminiscent of the classic Swedish meatball, but still completely beef-based. This basic recipe is very flexible. If necessary or if inspiration strikes, beef can be replaced with game, but then thirty percent pork (with as high a fat content as possible) should be added, because wild game meat is low in fat.

Naturally, not all recipes will start with these three basic recipes. But rest assured, they will all prove practical in your meatball-making journey.

THE MEDITERRANEAN FAMILY

GROUND MEAT – OFTEN WITH ELEMENTS OF VEAL FROM THE FRENCH AND ITALIAN KITCHENS, AND LAMB FROM THE TURKISH AND GREEK ONES – SHOULD BE GROUND FINER THAN TRADITIONAL SWEDISH GRIND. IF THE CHOICE IS MADE TO USE VEAL, IT MAY BE WISE TO ADD SOME EXTERNAL FAT: CREAM INSTEAD OF MILK IN THE BREADCRUMBS, FINELY CHOPPED BACON, OR EVEN LARD. IT'S NOT AT ALL CERTAIN THAT THE ENTIRETY OF FAT WILL STAY IN THE BALLS, BUT IT'S WELL WORTH A TRY.

BASIC RECIPE WITH GROUND VEAL:

1 kg ground veal, new and finely ground . . . .
1 dl breadcrumbs . . . .
1.5 dl cream . . . .
2 eggs . . . .

No onions? No spices? No. Not yet. What is most important here is that the ingredients used to season the meatball give it its character. And those ingredients will be listed in each recipe we mention.

THE ASIAN FAMILY

THE CONDITIONS FOR MAKING MEATBALLS ARE QUITE DIFFERENT
ON THE OTHER SIDE OF THE WORLD. HERE WE WORK WITH RICE,
PORK, COCONUT MILK AND A DASH OF SOY SAUCE.

BASIC ASIAN RECIPE:

1 kg ground pork – fresh and medium ground . . .

2 dl cooked rice . . . .

2 eggs . . . .

1 tbsp soy sauce (preferably from the country the
recipe is inspired by) . . . .

1-1.5 dl coconut . . . .

Here we replace breadcrumbs with cooked rice.
Rice binds fat almost better than bread. Despite
working with ground pork, we recommend using
coconut milk with a high fat content, mostly for
quality reasons: lighter types of coconut milk simply
contain more water, which won't be a crowd pleaser
when making meatballs. Pork can be substituted
with poultry without otherwise altering the ingredients. Asian meatballs are smaller and can generally
be "drier" balls as they often sit and simmer in
soups, woks and other pot-like dishes.

THE BEEF FAMILY

HERE, THE JOURNEY BEGINS WITH NEW VARIATIONS ON WHAT
SWEDES PERCEIVE AS THE TRADITIONAL MEATBALL.

BASIC RECIPE WITH GROUND BEEF:

1 kg ground beef – medium ground . . . .

1 dl breadcrumbs. . . . .

1.5 dl whole milk . . . .

2 eggs . . . .

This is a stripped-down version of the classic
Swedish meatball recipe. We present this simply to
make it possible to vary the classic recipe further
with different interesting ingredients.

IN OTHER PARTS OF THE WORLD

SOUTH INDIAN MEATBALLS
(Lamb, chicken and goat)

THIS RECIPE HAS THREE MAIN INGREDIENTS.
SIMPLY SUBSTITUTE LAMB WITH GROUND CHICKEN OR GOAT.

INGREDIENTS:

800 g ground lamb – fresh and medium ground

2 eggs . . . .

1 tbsp soy sauce (preferably from the country the recipe is inspired by) . . . .

0.5 dl coconut milk . . . .

Couscous . . . .

Salt, pepper . . . .

Cumin . . . .

DIRECTIONS:

Cook the couscous so that it amounts to 100 g when completely cooked. We cannot say exactly how much dry couscous you'll need because different varieties soak up different amounts of water, but use as granular a couscous as possible. In India, we replace the breadcrumbs with couscous. Let the couscous cool and mix with ground lamb. Add salt, pepper, 1 tbsp ground cumin and 0.5 dl coconut milk (this is certainly not the easiest variety of meatball to make).

If you use ground goat, add just over 1 tbsp ground ginger to reduce the typically unfamiliar taste of goat. Fry on low heat. Avoid burning the meatballs when using goat as a base; they'll taste particularly bad if you burn them. Make your own spice mix from scratch with Garam Masala (a spice mixture, but we'll skip the details for now), garlic, cumin, ginger, cayenne pepper, and lemon juice.

First, toast the cumin seeds in a pan until they produce a strong aroma. Boil the garlic in unsalted water for one minute. Finely grate the ginger and cook it in the oven at 120 degrees until dry, or use dried and ground ginger from your local store. Crush equal amounts of the spices in a mortar so they become a paste. Then add lemon juice, a few drops at a time, until you get a good balance between strength, saltiness and acidity. You can cheat a little by adding muscovado sugar – just know that's something an Indian housewife would never do. Or, buy a pre-made tandoori spice blend, preferably in paste form.

(While the cayenne pepper's on the countertop, anyway: did you know that you can cause respiratory arrest in any cook who happens to be in the kitchen by throwing a handful of cayenne pepper in a scalding hot frying pan or directly into the flame of a gas stove? During his time as a cooking student, Claes Grahn-Moller played practical jokes such as sending up a heated pan in the dumbwaiter just after throwing a massive handful of cayenne pepper into it. The dinner serving staff was quite amused, but it resulted in the fire department coming and the entire restaurant being evacuated.)

BOMBAY MEATBALLS

TANDOORI SEASONING ADAPTED TO A SWEDISH CONTEXT
ESPECIALLY INSPIRES THESE MEATBALLS.

INGREDIENTS:

1 kg lamb. . . . .

1.5 dl cream . . . .

1 dl breadcrumbs . . . .

2 eggs . . . .

TANDOORI SEASONING:

2 tbsp ground coriander . . . .

2 tbsp ground cumin . . . .

2 tsp ground cinnamon . . . .

1 tsp ground cloves. . . . .

1 tsp grated fresh ginger . . . .

3 tsp crushed garlic . . . .

2 tsp turmeric . . . .

1 tsp ground black pepper . . . .

1 tsp ground cardamom . . . .

1 tsp paprika powder . . . .

2 tsp cayenne pepper . . . .

1 tsk freshly grated nutmeg . . . .

DIRECTIONS:

Put on your favorite Indian music. The more sitar, the better. (Something that always gets us going is Anoushka Shankar's version of Pancham Se Gara. To roll the meatballs in time with the music is a challenge even for a rhythmic genius.)

Mix the bread and liquor separately with soft, harmonious movements, thoughtfully blending in the rest of the ingredients on their own and then stirring together when the liquid-bread mixture has bunched together like Bombay traffic on a Saturday afternoon.

BEVERAGE TIPS:

To accompany this, we drink Kingfisher – a bright, Indian lager that matches the spicy style of a tikka masala.

MASAI MARA MEATBALLS

THIS RECIPE IS (AS THE NAME SUGGESTS) INSPIRED BY THE
AUTHORS' TRAVELS IN AFRICA AND ESPECIALLY KENYA'S
BEAUTIFUL NATIONAL PARK MASAI MARA.

INGREDIENTS:

1 kg ground goat meat. . . . .

1.5 dl cream . . . .

1 dl breadcrumbs . . . .

2 eggs . . . .

1 tbsp cornstarch . . . .

1 tbsp sugar . . . .

1 tbsp coriander. . . . .

1 tbsp cinnamon . . . .

2 tsp mortar-crushed fennel seeds . . . .

2 tsp turmeric . . . .

2 tbsp grated ginger. . . . .

1 crushed clove garlic . . . .

1 tsp cumin . . . .

2 tsp mortar-crushed fenugreek seeds . . . .

DIRECTIONS:

These meatballs should harmonize on a serving
plate like a wildebeest herd, constantly following
the leader, with garlic and ginger in the mixture as a
reminder of ever-present wild animals. Mix the bread
first and the liquid separately until the mixture is
the consistency of mud at a watering hole. Stir the
remaining ingredients together and mix the two batters. Fry gently; ground goat can taste completely
worn-out and tired otherwise.

BEVERAGE TIP:

To accompany this we naturally drink Tusker lager,
a light beer from Kenya that harkens back to Masai
Mara and easily rinses away any dust stuck in one's
throat.

ROMAN MEATBALLS

INSPIRED BY MARCUS GAVIUS APICIUS' FIRST RECIPE.

INGREDIENTS:

0.5 kg ground lamb . . . .

0.5 kg ground beef . . . .

1 dl crushed *skorpor* (a Swedish style biscotti) or
other dry white bread . . . .

1.5 dl red wine . . . .

2 tsp black pepper . . . .

2 tsp garum (recipe below) or alternatively
Vietnamese nuoc mam or Thai nam pla . . . .

2 tbsp myrtle berries . . . .

DIRECTIONS:

Mix all ingredients above into small balls. If desired, add ground pepper and pine nuts.

Place the finished meatballs in a pan (Romans actually placed their meatballs in the connective tissue of the animal's stomach) and let them simmer in wine.

GARUM SAUCE:

Garum is a traditional Roman fish sauce used in many of the traditional recipes from this epoch. A contemporary counterpart can be made in the following way:

100 g anchovy fillets . . . .

50 g salt . . . .

1 pinch of oregano . . . .

1 pinch of mint . . . .

3 dl water . . . .

DIRECTIONS:

Bring everything to a boil, then let simmer for fifteen minutes under a closed lid. Use a wooden spoon to grind down any fish bits that are stuck together. Let simmer another fifteen minutes or until the liquid has boiled down. Strain the mixture (removing the liquid) through a fine sieve into a suitable container. Allow to cool. You're finished! Thanks to the high salt content, garum will last a long time in the refrigerator.

BEVERAGE TIP:

This recipe's heritage leaves us no choice: we choose the Italian wine Villa Bella Amarone. The wine is from the Valpolicella and made from grapes dried for 120 days, giving complexity and residual sweetness that harmonizes with the Italian spices and the nuoc mam's exotic style.

EXCLUSIVE MEATBALLS

MEATBALLS IN THESE RECIPES ARE OF A MORE
EXCLUSIVE KIND. MAKE THEM SLIGHTLY LARGER
THAN THE STANDARD RECIPES (WITH THE
EXCEPTION OF THE PUFF PASTRY-BAKED ONES).

TRUFFLE MEATBALLS

INGREDIENTS:

1 kg ground veal, fresh and finely ground. . . . . . .

1 dl breadcrumbs. . . . .

1.5 dl cream . . . .

2 eggs . . . .

1 truffle . . . .

2 shallots . . . .

Port wine . . . .

DIRECTIONS:

Chop 1 small truffle into approximately 2 mm-sized pieces (buy small truffles preserved in a can. Don't go and buy fresh truffles for hundreds of dollars). Chop 2 shallots.

Sauté the truffles and shallots in butter without letting the mixture color. Add about 1 dl port wine and let it reduce by half. Allow to cool and mix in the ground meat.

Roll the meatballs and fry. A more exclusive potato purée made with butter and cream can accompany these, as can a dark port wine sauce.

BEVERAGE TIP:

Go down into the cellar and get that old, well rounded Bordeaux. Find an old Chateau Haut-Brion or Château Palmer, decant nicely and astound your guests by serving a wine like this with your meatballs.

FOIE GRAS MEATBALLS

INGREDIENTS:

1 kg ground veal, fresh and finely ground . . . .

1 dl breadcrumbs . . . .

1.5 dl cream . . . .

2 eggs . . . .

Duck liver terrine or duck liver pâté . . . .

Cognac . . . .

DIRECTIONS:

Buy ready-made duck liver terrine or duck liver pâté. Cut into very small pieces. It doesn't matter if they're unequal in size, they'll still dissolve in the meat batter. Mix into the meat batter. Then add 4 cl of good cognac, the finer the better! Fry.

We recommend an easy, tasty salad as an accoutrement because the meatballs have a tendency to taste a little on the fatty side. Make your favorite salad and prepare a dressing as follows: Boil 1 egg for one minute, slice it in half, scrape out the white and yolk into a bowl. Pour in 2 tbsp cider vinegar, 1 tsp Dijon mustard, season with salt and pepper, and mix until it is smooth. Add 1 dl cold-pressed rapeseed oil and mix until you have a creamy consistency. Chop 1 green apple, 1 shallot, and a little parsley, mix in and stir. Dress the salad with the dressing, add the meatballs and finish with a little dressing on each ball.

BEVERAGE TIP:

Try a cold Sauternes! It's less crazy than it sounds. Pour the wine into a large, generous, preferably chilled glass and (naturally) keep the bottle cold in the fridge. Tips: try Château Suduiraut. If you can't handle the combination of Sauternes, drink champagne!

DUCK CONFIT

INGREDIENTS:

1 kg ground veal, fresh and finely ground . . . .

1 dl breadcrumbs . . . .

1.5 dl cream . . . .

2 eggs . . . .

Duck confit . . . .

DIRECTIONS:

Confit of duck is a very common spread in France. Buy it ready-made or do it yourself with duck leg and duck fat. It's easier than you think. Tell your butcher what you're planning so he gives you just the right amount of duck fat to cook with. The duck leg should be cooked in the duck fat for quite a long time – until the meat falls off the bones. Much like pulled pork.

Remove the meat from the pan, chop it up and mix it with the fat so that it becomes a thick paste. Pour the fat in little by little so that it avoids becoming too soupy. Now pour the batter into a mold and let cool in the refrigerator.

Mix 150 g of foie gras confit into the meat batter. This will make a bit more food than the usual recipe for 4 people, but it's so good that no one will complain!

A salad makes a great side dish to accompany this. Prep your favorite salad and make a dressing as follows: squeeze the juice of 1 orange and 0.5 lemon, chop 1 shallot and a little basil. While stirring, mix in 1 dl cold-pressed rapeseed oil and season with salt and pepper. Dress the salad by using what's left in the bowl to coat the meatballs. Serve with a rustic, light bread.

BEVERAGE TIP:

For this dish, drink a Belgian Ichtegems Grand Cru Cuvée.

MORELS

INGREDIENTS:

1 kg ground veal, fresh and finely ground. . . . . . .

1 dl breadcrumbs . . . .

1.5 dl cream . . . .

2 eggs . . . .

Dried morels . . . .

2 shallots . . . .

Madeira wine . . . .

DIRECTIONS:

Buy morels, preferably dried, and parboil by boiling them for 5 minutes in unsalted water. Grab a small handful of dried morels, parboil and then chop into approximately 2 mm sized pieces. Chop 2 shallots.

Sauté the morels and shallots in butter without letting them color. Add about 1 dl Madeira and let the liquid reduce by half. Roll the meatballs, fry and eat.

A well-suited accoutrement to these meatballs is a good potato purée with fresh vegetables such as broccoli, carrots and radish.

Split the broccoli into nice florets, and cut the carrot and radish into little fingertip-sized pieces. Boil plenty of well-salted water (a handful of salt for each 1 liter of water). Bring the water to a rolling boil. Melt 50g of butter in a pan that comfortably holds all the vegetables. Chop or finely slice 2 shallots, and let soften without coloring the butter.

Add the vegetables to the rolling, boiling salty water. Boil for 1 minute, drain in a colander, and put the vegetables in the butter and onion mixture immediately, stirring thoroughly but gently.

Pour the remaining buttered vegetable mixture (now to be used as a sauce for this dish) over the meatballs.

BEVERAGE TIP:

Beverage-wise, we're at a crossroads. A lighter IPA such as Sitting Bulldog IPA works well, but an even better choice might be Ojai Santa Barbara Chardonnay. Yes, a glass of white goes fantastically with morel meatballs.

BACON AND DIJON MUSTARD

INGREDIENTS:

1 kg ground veal, fresh and finely ground . . . .

1 dl breadcrumbs . . . .

1.5 dl cream . . . .

2 eggs . . . .

150 g of bacon . . . .

2 shallots

1.5 tbsp Dijon mustard . . . .

DIRECTIONS:

The idea here is to sauté the bacon and the shallots together. If the shallots get some color, don't worry – but sauté slowly. And don't use anything close to wok temperature on the pan!

Buy any cut of bacon at your local butcher. Bacon bought there has significantly lower water content than the plastic-wrapped, store bought kind. If you find yourself with plastic-wrapped bacon, increase the amount of bacon to 185 g.

Finely chop 2 shallots. Cut the bacon with kitchen shears (or slice, your choice) into centimeter-sized pieces. Sauté the onion and bacon until they start to show a nice color. Pour about half the fat in the frying pan and add 1.5 tbsp of Dijon mustard. (If available, use Grey Poupon to achieve the intended flavor strength of the recipe.) If you choose another mustard, decide for yourself what amount is right. On the other hand, you should always taste-test from time to time so you can moderate the amount of mustard yourself. Stir with a wooden spoon until blended.

Then mix with the meat batter, roll into balls and fry.

Freshly boiled new potatoes and really fresh vegetables such as broccoli, green beans and peas accompany these juicy and flavorful meatballs best. Divide the broccoli into florets. Boil plenty of well-salted water (use a handful of salt to 1 liter of water). Bring the water to a rolling boil. Melt 50 g of butter in a pan that generously holds the vegetables. Hack or fine-slice 2 shallots and let soften without coloring the butter. Add the vegetables to the rolling boiling salty water and boil for 45 seconds. Drain in a colander and immediately place the vegetables in the butter and shallot mixture. Stir thoroughly but gently. Top off with a stalk of finely shredded basil. Pour it all over the freshly boiled new potatoes, add the meatballs on top, and enjoy!

BEVERAGE TIP:

A cold beer suits these meatballs perfectly. Don't go with something mass-produced; rather, grab a few bottles of Bedarö Bitter made by Nynäshamns Ångbryggeri.

PUFF PASTRY BAKED MEATBALLS WITH ROQUEFORT

MANY NONPROFESSIONAL CHEFS ARE INTIMIDATED BY THE MERE THOUGHT OF WORKING WITH PUFF PASTRIES, BUT THIS IS OFTEN UNWARRANTED. IT IS TIME CONSUMING WORK, YES, BUT IT'S NOT A DIFFICULT TASK. THIS RECIPE HAS BEEN DESIGNED BY JEAN MILLET, PRESIDENT OF THE CONFEDERATION DE LA PATISSERIE, CINFISERIE, GLACERIE DE FRANCE, AND MOF IN PATISSERIE. THE RECIPE MAKES ABOUT 1.2 KG OF PUFF PASTRY. IT CAN BE FROZEN WITH GREAT RESULTS.

INGREDIENTS:

1 kg ground veal, new and finely ground . . . .

1 dl breadcrumbs . . . .

1.5 dl cream . . . .

2 eggs . . . .

Puff pastry (see opposite) . . . .

DIRECTIONS:

Make meatballs according to the recipe for Mediterranean meat batter, but don't fry them. Roll them to a somewhat smaller size. Cut squares out of the puff pastry, about 10x10 cm in size. Add a 1/2 cm thick slice of Roquefort, and add a raw meatball on top. Fold the puff pastry over and pinch the pastry edges firmly. Cut or trim excess pastry. Expect to serve 3-4 meatballs per person.

Place puff pastry pieces with the smooth side up (folds down), on a buttered plate or parchment paper. Brush with fresh cream. Bake in the oven at 200 degrees for about 9-10 minutes. Finished!

BEVERAGE TIP:

Naturally, one's first instinct is to pour a powerful wine that will match the cheese. Do so if you choose, but we think you should try a porter instead! Consider Butter Pound Porter, or the slightly different Grebbestads Oysters Porter.

PUFF PASTRY

INGREDIENTS:

500 g of wheat flour and a little more to add by hand

2 dl water . . . .

2 tsp salt . . . .

1/4 dl white wine vinegar. . . . .

50 g melted, unsalted butter . . . .

400 g unsalted butter, well chilled . . . .

DIRECTIONS:

Put 500 g of flour on the work surface and make a hole in the middle. Pour in the water, salt, vinegar and melted butter. Work it in using your fingertips. Use your left hand to gradually churn the flour into the batter and mix well.

When all the ingredients are fully blended, work the dough with the palm of your hand until it's completely smooth, but not too firm. Roll it into a ball and slice a cross on top. Then wrap the dough in plastic wrap and place in the refrigerator for 2-3 hours.

Lightly flour the work surface. Using a rolling pin, roll out 4 dough balls so that it looks like four big ears around a little head. Pound the cold butter several times with your rolling pin so that it stays soft but still remains very cold. Place the pounded butter on the head to fully cover it but without any excess hanging over the edges. Fold the four ears over the butter so that it is completely covered. Let stand in the fridge for 30 minutes.

Next, lightly flour the work surface again and roll out

the dough gently from the inside out so as to form a rectangle measuring 40x70 cm in size. Fold in the ends so that three layers are formed. This is the first round. In the second round, turn the rectangle a quarter-turn on the lightly floured work surface and gently roll it out again, from the inside and out, until you have a rectangle measuring 40x70 cm. Fold the dough in three parts. Wrap the dough in plastic wrap and leave it in the fridge for 30 minutes to harden. Continue in the same manner for an additional two rounds. Then wrap the dough and cool again for 30-60 minutes. Repeat the entire procedure two more times so that the total adds up to 6 rounds. The dough is now ready for use. As an alternative, we suggest going to your local dealer and purchasing ready-made puff pastry.

MEATBALLS FROM THE MEDITERRANEAN SEA

ALL THE RECIPES IN THIS SECTION ARE IDEAL TO SERVE WITH ANY
TYPE OF PASTA OR, IF YOU HAVE TIME, A GOOD RISOTTO.

ITALIAN MEATBALLS

ITALY HAS BECOME THE MEATBALL PROMISED LAND. THE PEOPLE'S ENJOYMENT OF FOOD, COMBINED WITH THE MANY DIFFERENT REGIONAL CUISINES (AND ESPECIALLY THE MELTING POT OF INFLUENCES THAT CAME OUT OF AMERICAN MIGRATION) HAS GIVEN ITALIAN CUISINE A UNIQUE POSITION IN MEATBALL CIRCLES.

INGREDIENTS:

1 kg ground veal . . . .

1.5 dl cream . . . .

1 dl breadcrumbs . . . .

2 eggs . . . .

1 dl finely chopped sundried tomatoes
(preserved in olive oil) . . . .

4 tbsp finely chopped Tuscan olives . . . .

2 tbsp finely chopped scallions . . . .

2 cloves garlic . . . .

1 tsp sage . . . .

2 tbsp finely grated pecorino cheese . . . .

DIRECTIONS:

Don't recoil when you see this mountain of ingredients; the actual preparation is pretty status quo. However, since we're going to be working with veal as well as many other ingredients, it can pay to make the meatballs a little smaller than traditional ones. This makes them hold together without burning. Free-hand salters, tempted to salt their meatballs "off recipe," should remember that even pecorino contributes an amount of saltiness.

BEVERAGE TIP:

Boira Sangiovese. An organic, fresh, lovely wine from Marche with notes of red berries and fresh acid that counters the creamy ground meat.

ISTANBULL KOFTE

THESE MEATBALLS CONTAIN LAMB AND ARE PREPARED IN THE
TYPICAL TURKISH FASHION.

INGREDIENTS:

1 kg ground lamb . . . .

1.5 dl goat's milk . . . .

1 dl breadcrumbs . . . .

2 eggs . . . .

4 minced garlic cloves . . . .

3 tbsp finely chopped parsley . . . .

1 tbsp finely chopped coriander . . . .

1 tsp ground cumin . . . .

0.5 tsp cinnamon . . . .

0.5 tsp ground ginger . . . .

0.5 tsp black pepper . . . .

DIRECTIONS:

This is a recipe for big meatballs, at least 4 cm in
circumference, which are fried in olive oil and butter.
Serve with vegetable rice and mint yogurt.

BEVERAGE TIP:

Sade Öküzgözü is made from the grape Öküzgözü
from Turkey and is a fruity, red wine with notes of
berries that goes well with lamb.

HOT COALS

RED-HOT MEATBALLS SERVED ON FIRE, IS IT POSSIBLE? OF COURSE!
THIS DISH IS A PARTY STARTER. MOREOVER, YOU SHOULDN'T EVER MISS
AN OPPORTUNITY TO FLAMBÉ, RIGHT?

INGREDIENTS:

1 kg ground beef – medium ground
1 dl breadcrumbs
1.5 dl whole milk
2 eggs
3 tbs ayvar relish
1 red chili, finely chopped (remove the seeds)
Salt and pepper to taste

DIRECTIONS:

Where do we start? The batter, of course.
Then cook the meatballs normally. When they are ready, it's time for the grand finale. Place the balls in a sauté pan, then place the pan on the stove so that it gets really hot. Douse with 3 cl slivovitz and (keeping a safe distance from the stove fan, naturally) light it on fire.
Shake the pan until the meatballs extinguish. Serve to applause.

ACCESSORIES:

Because this recipe has ancient Yugoslavian roots, we think of trimmings that match:
Shoestring fried potatoes
Sour cream (or smetana)
Chopped raw yellow onion

BEVERAGE TIP:

Naturally, offer your guests slivovitz to accompany the food. We recommend Prior Slivovka Plum; or, just rummage in the cupboard and see if there's any liquor left over from your college days. Drink Dugges Barliner with raspberry flavor if you dare, otherwise a Slovenian Lasko Club might be just right.

SUNDRIED TOMATOES IN OIL AND PARMESAN CHEESE

INGREDIENTS:

1 kg ground veal, new and finely ground . . . .

1 dl breadcrumbs . . . .

1.5 dl cream . . . .

2 eggs . . . .

Sundried tomatoes . . . .

Parmesan . . . .

DIRECTIONS:

Take 7-8 pieces of dried tomatoes that have been preserved in oil and finely chop them. Pour the chopped tomatoes and 1 dl of coarsely grated Parmesan cheese in the ground meat. Mix in a bit of the oil the tomatoes had been stored in, but not too much, so that the meat batter starts to fall apart.

BEVERAGE TIP:

A soft wine from Sicily is perfect! Since you prepared your meatballs with organic ingredients, choose the organically-grown Raccolto Nero d'Avola Cabernet Sauvignon.

MOZZARELLA, BASIL AND GARLIC

INGREDIENTS:

1 kg ground veal, fresh and finely ground . . . . . .

1 dl breadcrumbs . . . .

1.5 dl cream . . . .

2 eggs . . . .

Mozzarella . . . .

Fresh basil . . . .

3 cloves garlic . . . .

DIRECTIONS:

This is an example of meatballs that can be successfully braised with a good tomato sauce!

Take 1 large mozzarella ball or two smaller ones (equaling 80-100 g). Select a mozzarella of good quality (such as buffalo mozzarella), preferably organic. Take an entire basil plant or a large bunch from the garden or balcony planting pot.

Cook the garlic cloves 1 minute in unsalted water. Mince the garlic. Dice the mozzarella into 0.5 cm pieces. Shred the basil; you don't have to be too fancy here -larger pieces are totally acceptable. Blend everything into the ground meat and be sure not to turn the heat up so high that it will burn the brittle basil leaves (which might throw off the flavor).

BEVERAGE TIP:

Choose super expensive and tasty Brunello di Montalcino or a lightweight like Brolio for maximum Tuscan feel.

LARDO AND OLIVES

INGREDIENTS:

1 kg ground veal, fresh and finely ground . . . . . .
1 dl breadcrumbs . . . .
1.5 dl cream . . . .
2 eggs . . . .
150 g olives . . . .
200 g of lardo . . . .

DIRECTIONS:

Feel free to use your favorite olives, naturally. However, we strongly recommend Italian Cerignola olives. Look for them in your store – the taste will be worth it.

Lardo is cured pig fat. It's the coat of fat from the pig's back. It's incredibly good when used correctly. Ask your butcher to cut lardo much like bacon slices, and wrap each meatball in a slice.

In addition you'll need a little bit (about 50 g) to fry along with the olives.

Seed and chop the olives. Sauté them together with 50 g diced lardo over medium heat, without flat-out frying them.

Pour out the fat from the pan, but keep 2 tbsp and mix everything into the meat batter. Now comes the mouth-watering part! Take a raw meatball and wrap a slice of lardo around it. The slice should overlap a little. Now place the meatball in the hot pan with the wrap seam-side down, pressing it down for a few seconds. At this point, the ends of the lardo slice should have joined together neatly, so you can let go of the meatball and let it roll around wherever it wants in the pan. Do the same with all the meatballs. Fry until golden.

BEVERAGE TIP:

This dish is both fatty and salty tasting, so you may want to have one (or many) Peroni Nastro Azzurro to wash the meatballs down. You can also opt for a light Italian Chianti and refrigerate it for half an hour before serving.

SALVIA (like saltimbocca)

INGREDIENTS:

1 kg fresh veal, new and finely ground . . . .

1 dl breadcrumbs . . . .

1.5 dl cream . . . .

2 eggs . . . .

Fresh sage . . . .

1 clove garlic . . . .

DIRECTIONS:

Grab an entire bunch of sage, or at least a large handful of stalks, from your balcony planter or garden. We want to use whole leaves, which requires some dexterity – but it's worth it. Pluck all the leaves from the stalks. Finely chop the garlic and mix everything into the meat batter. Be careful when you fry it, but don't worry if the sage leaves color a bit. Sage, unlike basil, is fine even when colored.

BEVERAGE TIP:

Serve your guests Semillon in large red wine glasses.

ANCHOVIES, COPPA AND LEMON

INGREDIENTS:

1 kg ground veal, new and finely ground . . . .

1 dl breadcrumbs . . . .

1.5 dl cream . . . .

2 eggs . . . .

80 g anchovies . . . .

80 g Coppa . . . .

0.5 lemon . . . .

DIRECTIONS:

Coppa is salted and cured pork loin, and you buy it ready-made at your local butcher. Chop the anchovies and coppa and mix into the ground veal. Rinse and finely grate the skin of half a lemon and mix into the veal. Make small meatballs and serve as snacks. These taste great even when cold. And they're divinely good without any sauce at all!

BEVERAGE TIP:

Drink whatever you want! Or what your guests want. When it comes to finding a beverage that goes with anchovies, it's a challenge. But we recommend a rosé, like Grande Recolte, which makes for a pleasant time, regardless. What's more, the square bottle is a nice novelty.

MEATBALL CALZONE

AN INSANE DISH. DON'T ATTEMPT THIS DISH IF YOU DON'T HAVE AN OVEN THAT CAN PROVIDE 300 DEGREE HEAT AND HAS A STONE BASE. MOREOVER, IT'S A GOOD DISH — BUT RARELY PRETTY. START BY MAKING REGULAR PIZZA DOUGH:

INGREDIENTS:

0.5 package yeast . . . .

2 dl lukewarm water . . . .

1 tbsp oil . . . .

5 dl flour . . . .

0.5 tsp salt . . . .

2 shallots . . . .

1 clove garlic . . . .

2 tbsp tomato paste . . . .

1 can of pureed tomatoes . . . .

Mozzarella . . . .

Select an Italian meatball recipe of your choice, cook accordingly.

DIRECTIONS:

Dissolve the yeast in warm water, mix in the remaining ingredients and let rise for 8-10 minutes. Roll out on a floured surface and get started.

Make a tomato sauce with 2 chopped shallots and 1 finely chopped garlic clove. Fry the onion on low heat so it doesn't color and the garlic doesn't burn. If it does, throw everything away and start over. Add 2 tbsp tomato puree and 1 can of crushed tomatoes. Let reduce down to half. Season with salt, sugar and pepper.

Make pieces of dough large enough so that you can fit 4-5 meatballs inside them. Spread the tomato sauce on one half of the dough with a wooden spoon. Place the meatballs in a row and add generous slices of mozzarella. Fold the dough over to make a semi-circle. Pinch the edges closed – do not use a fork because it will risk destroying the dough.

Bake at 320 degrees for 6-8 minutes or until the pizza is golden. Ask the family to keep their fingers crossed that the filling doesn't break free and leak into the oven. If it does, it'll look horrible, but it'll taste just as good, regardless.

BEVERAGE TIP:

Drink whatever you usually drink when eating pizza. We recommend a lightly chilled, simple Italian wine you drink in a normal glass. Buy a box of The Big Zin Zinfandel Old Wines and place in the fridge while you bake your pizza.

ALBÓNDIGAS

INGREDIENTS:

1 kg ground veal, fresh and finely ground . . . . . .

1 dl breadcrumbs . . . .

1.5 dl cream . . . .

2 eggs . . . .

4 cloves garlic . . . .

1 green pepper . . . .

1 red pepper . . . .

1 bunch fresh parsley leaves . . . .

Paprika powder . . . .

Piementón de la Vera or cayenne pepper and

chipotle paste . . . .

1 kg whole, preserved Spanish tomatoes . . . .

3 chopped yellow onions . . . .

0.5 dl of Spanish olive oil . . . .

3 tbsp chili sauce of good quality . . . .

1 tbsp sherry vinegar . . . .

0.5 flowerpot fresh oregano . . . .

2 tbsp honey . . . .

2 dl good sherry, the best you have at home . . .

Salt and pepper . . . .

DIRECTIONS:

Start by making the sauce. It'll be good to let it stand and mingle together while you're struggling with your albóndigas. Grab a big pot that will fit all the albóndigas plus the tomato sauce. Take the whole tomatoes, 2 chopped onions, olive oil, chili sauce, sherry vinegar, oregano, honey and sherry (pour a glass for yourself right now). Throw everything in the pot and boil gently. Add salt and pepper. Season to taste. Now imagine the Spanish sun and the country's landscape. Taste the sauce. Do we need to add anything else? When you feel satisfied, lower the heat and let the sauce simmer with the lid on.

These meatballs are based on the recipe for Mediterranean meat batter. Chop 4 cloves garlic, 1 onion, 1 green pepper and 1 red pepper. Coarsely chop the whole bunch of leafy parsley, and set it aside. It will be added towards the end.

Fry the onion and bell pepper over medium heat without letting it color. Add 1 tsp paprika powder, 2 pinches Piementón de la Vera or 1 pinch cayenne pepper, and 1 pinch chipotle paste and fry for a moment. Add the chopped parsley and remove the pan from the heat. Now mix everything with the ground meat and shape into large meatballs – as big as tennis balls. Fry them so they take on a nice color but not so much so that they cook fully. They'll get finished in the tomato sauce. Now add the meatballs to the pan containing the sauce, turn up the heat and let it all simmer, covered, for 10-15 minutes. Keep track of time from the moment it begins to simmer – not from the moment you add the meatballs. Serve with good bread, Pour a glass of any wine from the Penedès and dream of Spain.

GREEK WITH CHEESE

INGREDIENTS:

400 g ground lamb . . . .

400 g ground beef . . . .

1 dl breadcrumbs . . . .

1.5 dl cream . . . .

2 eggs . . . .

200 g black olives . . . .

150 g Greek sheep cheese . . . .

DIRECTIONS:

Mix the ground lamb with the ground beef. Seed the olives, then finely chop and blend the meat batter. Coarsely chop your high quality Greek sheep cheese and mix together carefully. Stir gently – we want real pieces of cheese in the meatballs so avoid breaking them up too much. Roll into balls and fry as usual. Serve, as one would expect, with tzatziki and nothing more.

BEVERAGE TIP:

Maybe you should drink a Greek wine, but we think that an American is better. Buy a bottle of Buena Vista Sonoma Zinfandel. It costs a little more but it's worth it.

KEBAB SEASONED MEATBALLS ON SKEWERS

INGREDIENTS:

900 g ground lamb, fresh and finely ground . . . .

1 dl breadcrumbs . . . .

1.5 dl cream . . . .

2 eggs . . . .

1 onion . . . .

3 cloves garlic . . . .

1 fresh chili . . . .

0.5 bunch coriander . . . .

0.5 bunch parsley . . . .

0.5 bunch mint . . . .

Cumin . . . .

Black pepper . . . .

Salt . . . .

DIRECTIONS:

Cut an onion into 4 wedges and take 3 whole garlic cloves, half a bunch of coriander, half a bunch of leaf parsley and half a bunch of mint, 2 eggs, 1 tbsp cumin, 1 tsp black pepper, 1 tbsp stove cumin, 1 fresh chili (choose the type and strength you want) and a little salt: put everything in your blender or food processor. Run it until everything gets chopped up just enough and mixes together.

Blend the spice mix in the 800 g of finely ground lamb. Roll into balls and put on wooden skewers. Soak wooden skewers thoroughly before use. Now you can either cook over the briquettes or bake at 175 degrees for 6-10 minutes, depending on the size of the meatballs. Serve in a pita with lettuce, sliced onions, optional hot sauce and/or tzatziki.

BEVERAGE TIP:

For this dish you can opt for a standard glass of cold tap water or a good Turkish tea like Cay – strong, sweet and served hot in a glass. When the Ottoman Empire collapsed and coffee imports decreased, it's said that Atatürk urged his citizens in then newly-formed Turkey to drink more tea and less coffee. Boil water, throw in the tea, and let it sit for a long time, 15-20 minutes on low heat (do not boil). Then dilute with hot water to the desired strength and sweeten with any kind of sugar.

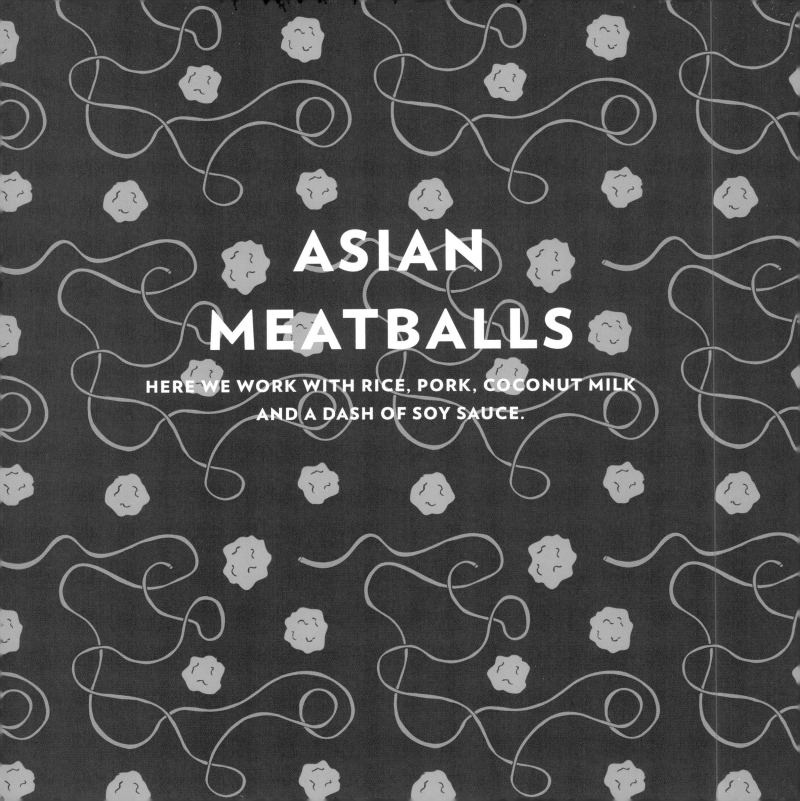

ASIAN MEATBALLS

HERE WE WORK WITH RICE, PORK, COCONUT MILK
AND A DASH OF SOY SAUCE.

NEM NOUNG

INGREDIENTS:

800 g coarsely ground pork . . . .

2 tbsps fish sauce . . . .

2 tbsps palm sugar . . . .

2 shallots . . . .

2 cloves garlic . . . .

DIRECTIONS:

Pour the fish sauce and palm sugar in a bowl. Stir until the sugar is dissolved. Finely chop the shallots and garlic. Blend into the ground pork. Roll into balls and fry gently on fairly high heat. Roll the meatballs frequently and thoroughly. The sugar makes it so the surfaces will burn slightly, which is good – just be careful not to let them burn too much.

BEVERAGE TIP:

A Vietnamese person wouldn't naturally choose this, but a dark lager goes better than you might think with these balls. Try a Störtebeker Schwarz-Bier.

MEATBALLS FROM THE FISHING VILLAGE OF MUI NE

INGREDIENTS:

400 g large, raw shrimp, such as jumbo shrimp (make sure you choose shrimp that are not on the endangered seafood list) . . . .

400 g finely ground chicken . . . .

1 egg . . . .

1 bunch coriander . . . .

1 tsp fresh ginger . . . .

1 fresh chili . . . .

1 tbsp fish sauce . . . .

1 clove garlic . . . .

Sesame seeds, black and white . . . .

DIRECTIONS:

Chop the shrimp thoroughly. Mix with finely ground chicken and 1 egg. Blend in a full bunch of chopped cilantro, 1 tsp finely grated fresh ginger, 1 small, finely chopped fresh chili (choose the variety and strength you want) and 1 tbsp fish sauce, preferably Vietnamese. Finely grate 1 garlic clove and mix with the meat batter. Shape into meatballs and roll them in the sesame seeds. If you want, you can roll half in black sesame seeds and half in white.

Time to heat the deep fryer to 150 degrees. If you don't have a deep fryer, get one. It's possible to deep-fry in a pan but for safety reasons we do not recommend it. You can also do what they do in Mui Ne – fry outdoors in a wok if you have a cooking plate with a powerful enough gas burner (over 9 kW).

BEVERAGE TIP:

Bia Hoi is the standard Vietnamese beer. It's cheap, simple and refreshing, with low alcohol content. Another worthy choice is Hanoi Beer. Otherwise, just about any other light and fresh lager will do.

SESAME BALLS

INGREDIENTS:

1 kg ground pork, fresh and medium ground . . . .

100 g peeled and chopped shrimp . . . .

100 g white fish (cod, haddock etc.), chopped .

1 tsp finely grated fresh ginger . . . .

0.5 bunch chopped coriander . . . .

1 chopped and deseeded red chili . . . .

2 dl cooked rice . . . .

2 eggs . . . .

1 tbsp soy sauce (optional, preferably from the recipe's country of origin) . . . .

1-1.5 dl coconut . . . .

FOR BREADING:

Sesame seeds . . . .

DIRECTIONS:

Roll the meatballs normally. After you get them the way you want them, put the balls in a small container filled with sesame seeds and shake.

Place them in a moderately hot skillet with about 1 cm of oil. The oil shouldn't boil or sizzle – just maintain a high temperature of about 140 degrees.

ACCESSORIES:

Mango and noodle salad

0.5 dl freshly squeezed lime juice . . . .

1 tbsp sugar . . . .

0.5 dl canola oil (or another flavor-neutral oil)

2 tbsp sesame oil . . . .

2 green mangoes (finely sliced into slivers) . . . .

1 packet noodles . . . .

0.5 bunch coriander . . . .

Boil the noodles, put them in a bowl and mix with the other ingredients.

BEVERAGE TIP:

You can pair a crisp Chablis with anything that has lime, mango, coriander and chili. There are many to choose from but we think you should grab a few bottles of Petit Chablis Domaine Sainte Claire. This small Chablis goes perfectly with these meatballs.

VIETNAMESE

INGREDIENTS:

800 g ground pork . . . .

1 egg . . . .

2 finely chopped shallots . . . .

2 cloves garlic . . . .

1 pinch ground cinnamon . . . .

1 small finely chopped, fresh chili . . . .

1 stalk finely chopped lemongrass . . . .

1 dl coconut milk . . . .

DIRECTIONS:

Mix the ground pork, eggs, finely chopped shallots, garlic cloves, cinnamon, chopped fresh chili (choose the variety and strength you want) and finely chopped lemongrass. Mix well. Then add the coconut milk (not the light kind) and blend together. Roll into balls.

Boil water in a large saucepan. When the water has boiled, add the meatballs and let them lie in the water under the lid for 4-6 minutes, depending on how large the meatballs are. They are fantastic to serve cold in a salad with pac choi, mango, cabbage and sliced and cooked bamboo shoots. Dress the salad with a few dashes of nuoc cham, mixed with a neutral-tasting oil.

BEVERAGE TIP:

Treat yourself to a really nice Pinot Noir from South Africa if you can afford it, like Chamonix Pinot Noir Reserve. It breaks nicely with the cinnamon, talks sweetly with the coconut milk, and takes the lemon grass out for a dance. Alternatively, drink Vietnamese tea! Your choice of Pekoe from northern Vietnam is ideal.

NOUC CHAM

(A standard dipping sauce that goes with all types of meatballs and more)

INGREDIENTS:

1 dl fish sauce . . . .

1 dl palm sugar . . . .

1.5 dl freshly squeezed lime . . . .

2 large garlic cloves . . . .

2 red chilies . . . .

DIRECTIONS:

Mix the fish sauce (preferably Vietnamese – yes, it *does* taste differently), palm sugar, fresh lime juice, finely chopped garlic cloves, and finely chopped, fresh chilies (choose the variety and strength you want). You don't have to be meticulous when removing the chilies – let a few seeds remain in the sauce. Heat the fish sauce, add the sugar and let it melt. Let cool and mix in the lime juice, chili and onions.

If the fish sauce flavor is too intense, dilute the sauce with water and balance it with more lime juice. Served cold as a dipping sauce.

GROUND BEEF MEATBALLS

MEATBALL PLANK

THE SWEDISH DISH PLANKSTEK IS A DISH APPROACHING CULT STATUS IN
ITS NATIVE COUNTRY. SO WHY NOT MAKE A MEATBALL VERSION INSPIRED
BY THE AUTHORS' VISITS TO THE STOCKHOLM RESTAURANT GODTHEM
DURING THE EARLY '80S?

INGREDIENTS:

1 kg ground beef – medium ground . . . .

1 dl breadcrumbs . . . .

1.5 dl whole milk . . . .

2 eggs . . . .

1 dl finely chopped, crispy bacon . . . .

0.5 dl finely chopped haricots verts. . . . .

You can't have a plank steak without béarnaise
sauce. And this makes it the ultimate sauce:

2 sliced shallots . . . .

0.5 dl red wine vinegar . . . .

4 crushed white peppercorns . . . .

0.5 bunch tarragon . . . .

0.5 dl water . . . .

Boil the above until about 3 tbsp of liquid remains. Strain the liquid in a new pan placed on
very low heat. Add 4 egg yolks and whisk until
light and airy.

Melt 400 g butter in another saucepan.

Pour the melted butter over the sauce (be careful
not to get any of the liquid in the bottom of the
butter – it's not fat) and add the other half bunch
of tarragon (also chopped) and a pinch of cayenne
pepper. Add salt to taste.

DIRECTIONS:

The plank should be a piece of oak 800 x 400 x
40mm in size, if one is picky. You'll naturally place the
meatballs and tomato on it, and pipe mashed potatoes around the edges as a finishing touch.

Cut the tomato's top and drip a mixture of butter
and breadcrumbs on it. Add the tomato next to the
meatballs and mashed potatoes.

The plank should be baked at 200 degrees in the
oven until the potatoes and tomatoes look finished.

Serve with béarnaise sauce on the side.

BEVERAGE TIP:

Enjoy with a classic Swedish lager like Pripps Blue.

HUGE, HOT-SMOKED
ELK MEATBALLS

SMOKED MEATBALLS? OF COURSE! RECREATION AND NUTRITION IN THE SAME BEAUTIFUL RECIPE.

INGREDIENTS:

1 kg ground elk meat, medium ground . . . .
1 dl breadcrumbs . . . .
1.5 dl whole milk . . . .
2 eggs . . . .
1.5 tbsp freshly grated ginger . . . .
Salt and pepper to taste . . . .

If you don't own your own hunting land, aren't a member of any hunting parties, don't know any hunters or don't even hunt, you can still make these meatballs. Depending on where in the world you are, elk can be found at your butcher during autumn and winter, but it can be harder to find during the rest of the year. In any case, you must have a kettle barbecue and birch logs (or a smoker and birch shavings) in which you can cook the meatballs.

This recipe takes about 90 minutes from start to finish, so be sure to start in good time before your guests' arrival. Before you begin, deck the table out with some pine branches; it makes for a nice presentation. Do not wear your expensive wool suit or favorite jeans when making this dish. You will be impregnated by birch log smoke.

DIRECTIONS:

Before you start with the meatballs, prepare the kettle barbecue. Fold the three layers of aluminum foil into a tray that takes up half the surface of your grill's bottom. Make sure the sides are 5-6 cm high (you can also buy ready-made aluminum trays if your store has them). Pour water into the tray, filling it as much as possible. Place a thin layer of briquettes in the second half of the grill bottom.

Break off a few twigs from 2-3 large birch logs and place the logs and twigs on top of the briquettes. Make sure you place the cooking grate on top of everything without the wood touching it.

Light the wood. If you have a butane torch in the kitchen, use that for quick and easy lighting – but never use lighter fluid. Now, leave the grill for a moment and go into the kitchen.

Make a meat batter according to the Classic Swedish Meatballs recipe but replace the ground meat with ground elk. Also, add 1 1/2 tbsp finely grated fresh ginger, and do not skimp on the black pepper. If you happen to have a good liquor at home, throw a few tbsp into the mixture. Roll the balls slightly smaller than the size of tennis balls.

Now pour yourself a beer and go out and check on the grill. Your birch should still be burning nicely – don't let it go out. If you only see glowing embers, you've spent too much time in the kitchen. Throw on another log. Take another swig of your brew. Gaze into the fire. Ponder deep things.

Now it's time to put more water in the aluminum pan. After that, put the cooking grate back and the grill cover on. Close the bottom vent on the grill completely. The wood will immediately extinguish when the vent is closed and beautiful smoke will puff out of the top vent and seep out around the lid's edges. Perfect! Now you're on your way! Go into the kitchen and pour yourself another beer. Put the meatballs on a wooden plank, go outside and place them on the cooking grate above the water tray. The wood will naturally flare up when you open the lid – that doesn't matter, it settles down when you put the lid back on.

The next step requires a little skill but you'll eventually get to know your firewood and grill for a perfect result every time: we have to regulate the temperature using the vent in the lid. Check the temperature by holding your hand in the smoke that's billowing out. The temperature of the smoke should ideally be 120-150 degrees (don't burn yourself!). That said, we're making elk meatballs so we're not being super careful here. Don't let the wood go out – that just makes things more complicated. If there starts to be problems with too little smoke, try opening the bottom vent. Or, lift the lid a little to get things moving with the wood again. Take a swig of beer, sit down and relax.

You'll need to move the meatballs around approximately every 15 minutes so each gets equal time close to the burning timber. Turn them with care if you think too much color is building up on the bottoms. Use your hands – barbecue tongs or spatulas hurt meatballs. Wear gloves if it gets too hot. If all your wood burns out, add a new log, let it burn for 4-5 minutes, place the grate back on the grill and cover.

After half an hour poke the meatballs a little bit to check how they feel. They are ready when their skin starts to feel solid. We can't give any exact timing for when your meatballs will be ready. It depends on how large you make them and what temperature you keep the grill at. But somewhere between 40-60 minutes should do.

Once you're happy with the meatballs, remove them, wrap them in aluminum foil and set them aside. Let rest for 10 minutes. Add some pine branches on the wooden plank, cut up the meatballs in centimeter-thick slices and add some more branches. These wonderful meatballs can be eaten with your fingers, just as they are. Or, why not make a chanterelle sauce and mashed potatoes and serve as a full meal? If you can get your hands on them, garnish with Swedish rårörda lingonberries, and naturally, have a shot (or many) of your favorite drink.

**SNACKS TO EAT WHILE
YOU'RE MAKING MEATBALLS:**

Crispbread
Freshly Ground Brisket
Salt
Black Pepper
Egg yolk

LOUISIANA HOT JAZZ MEATBALLS

EVEN JAZZ MUSICIANS HAVE TO EAT, AND THIS IS A DISH THAT IS APPRECIATED BY BLUES MUSICIANS OF ALL KINDS, ESPECIALLY SLIDE GUITAR PLAYERS.

INGREDIENTS:

1 kg ground beef . . . .
0.5 kg spicy chorizo . . . .
3 dl chopped shrimp tails . . . .
1 onion . . . .
1 dl chopped scallions . . . .
1 dl finely chopped red pepper . . . .
1 chopped celery stalk . . . .
5 chopped garlic cloves . . . .
2 tsp ground cinnamon . . . .
2 tsp chopped fresh mint . . . .
1 tsp ground cayenne pepper . . . .
1 tsp Worchestershire sauce (Lea & Perrins) . . .
1 tsp Tony Cachere's Cajun spice . . . .
2 eggs . . . .
4 tsp hot mustard . . . .
Tabasco as desired
Pepper and salt to taste . . . .
A splash of white wine to keep the shrimp tails happy
Olive oil . . . .
Butter . . . .

DIRECTIONS:

Sauté the onion, bell pepper, celery and garlic in a pan with olive oil and butter. After a little time has passed, add some white wine. Put the rest of the ingredients in a large bowl, pour the mixture all over them and mix well.

Roll the balls so they are 2.5 cm in size. If you roll them too big, you will destroy the shrimp tails.

Fry in olive oil and butter.

Serve with cornbread and red beans & rice.

BEVERAGE TIP:

Réserve de Bonnet Rosé – a food-friendly, fresh rosé from Bordeaux that works with savory chorizo, shrimp tails and strong flavors. Otherwise, Pabst Blue Ribbon and Corona with lime will work like a charm.

HEAVY METAL MEATBALLS

EVEN METAL HEADS HAVE TO GET THEIR MEATBALLS ON, AND THEY SHOULD BE LIKE THE STYLE OF MUSIC ITSELF: HEAVY, FULL-BODIED AND WITH DEEP ROOTS IN ALL THE FLAVORS ROCKERS APPRECIATE.

INGREDIENTS:

1 kg ground beef . . . .

4 tbsp Jack Daniel's Bourbon . . . .

1.5 dl Pabst Blue Ribbon . . . .

1 dl breadcrumbs . . . .

Tabasco – exactly how much to use is, of course, a matter of taste and a question of your pallet's courage. But for genuine metal-level strength you'll need to add at least 6-10 drops. In true metal tradition, Tabasco can be replaced with any of the myriad insanely hot sauces that will in-evitably grace the table when real gourmet metal heads meet and discuss food. And in terms of seasoning, the sky's the limit . . . .

Garlic is a standard ingredient in the metal kitchen. At least 4 cloves keep vampires away . .

Corn cobs, cut in 4 cm pieces . . . .

DIRECTIONS:

Make the batter just like the classic recipe.

Roll the balls a little bigger, about 4 cm in diameter.

Place on a buttered metal tray in the oven, 166.5 degrees (one quarter of 666) for ten minutes. The goal is to make them firm enough to be placed on skewers.

Skewer the meatballs on pre-soaked wooden skewers, alternating with pieces of corn on the cob.

Throw everything on the grill until the meatballs are nicely browned and pink in the middle. The temperature in the middle of the meatball should measure about 55 degrees.

Serve with generous amounts of barbecue sauce, coleslaw and baked potato.

BEVERAGE TIP:

For hard rock meatballs we drink Ravenswood Zinfandel, a red, full-bodied wine from California. And while you're in the meatball mix of it all, drink Jack Daniels as a fine pairing. Beer? Yes, Pabst Blue Ribbon is already chilling in the fridge.

THE FOUR SEASONS

THE MEATBALL IS ACTUALLY A FOOD FOR ANY SEASON. THAT'S ONE OF ITS ADVANTAGES. BUT NOTHING SHOULD STOP YOU FROM EXPERIMENTING WITH DIFFERENT SEASONINGS AND AC-CESSORIES TO TAILOR THE MEATBALL TO THE SEASON YOU'RE IN. THEREFORE, WE WOULD LIKE TO PROPOSE THE FOUR SEASONS WITH A FIFTH BONUS MEATBALL IN THE FORM OF A CHRISTMAS MEATBALL, AND EVEN A SIXTH – THE LUCIA MEATBALL – WHICH IS A MEATBALL HEAVILY INFLUENCED BY THE SWEDISH-STYLE CELEBRATION OF CHRISTMAS.

SPRING

A LITTLE LIGHTER MEATBALL.
FULL OF HOPE AND SPRINGTIME SPICES.

INGREDIENTS:

0.5 kg ground beef – medium ground . . . .

0.5 kg ground lamb . . . .

1 dl breadcrumbs . . . .

1.5 dl whole milk . . . .

2 eggs . . . .

A bundle of shredded wild garlic . . . .

A few sprigs of chopped, fresh rosemary . . . . . .

Serve with mashed potatoes (see recipe for mashed potatoes that go with traditional meatballs) and a few extra ingredients in the form of:

Garlic oil, about 2 tbsp . . . .

A bunch of finely chopped parsley . . . .

DIRECTIONS:

Inspired by flowers blooming and snow thawing, we're making meatballs slightly smaller than traditional ones. By now you've probably found your own personal style of frying meatballs. Make them that way – no funny business – just be sure to peel off any burnt rosemary pieces after frying. It's not a catastrophe if you don't, it's just more aesthetically pleasing.

   Good with:

   Grated parmesan cheese at a thickness you might get if grated with a wood planer – basically, as big as you would like your grated cheese normally. Place on a baking sheet covered with parchment paper and cook at 200 degrees in the oven until a toffee brown-colored surface appears. Carefully and quickly remove the chips from the paper so that they don't stick.

BEVERAGE TIP:

Pour yourself a Mikkeller American Dream so the foam froths in the glass. If you need a little extra warmth, try Helderberg Cabernet Sauvignon.

SUMMER

GREEN AND WARM IN THE SUN, BARBECUE SPICE WORKS AS A SUBSTITUTE FLAVOR FOR
THOSE WHO REALLY ONLY WANT TO EAT FLINTSTEAK (A BARBECUE-SPICED, LARGE CHUNK
OF PORK, POPULAR IN SWEDEN AND NAMED AFTER THE DIET OF THE FLINTSTONES).

INGREDIENTS:

1 kg ground beef, medium ground . . . .

1 dl breadcrumbs . . . .

1.5 dl whole milk . . . .

2 eggs . . . .

1 dl finely chopped chives . . . .

3 tbsp barbecue seasoning (any brand) . . . .

DIRECTIONS:

This is a straight-shooting meatball, well suited for after a hard day at the beach. Maybe you've made the batter and rolled the balls even before leaving the house for the day? The customary method of meatball cooking is in play here, but make sure that the finely chopped chives are truly finely chopped (use the kids to hack 'em if they are impatient) and that the barbecue spice is well-distributed in the batter.

Good with:

A baked potato or even roasted potatoes? Coleslaw (see the Heavy Metal Meatball recipe for how this is made)

And perhaps rhubarb pie for dessert?

BEVERAGE TIP:

A glass of ice-cold milk goes perfectly with these meatballs. But if you're looking for an adult beverage, try a Gambrinus or a big glass of Mulderbosch Rosé.

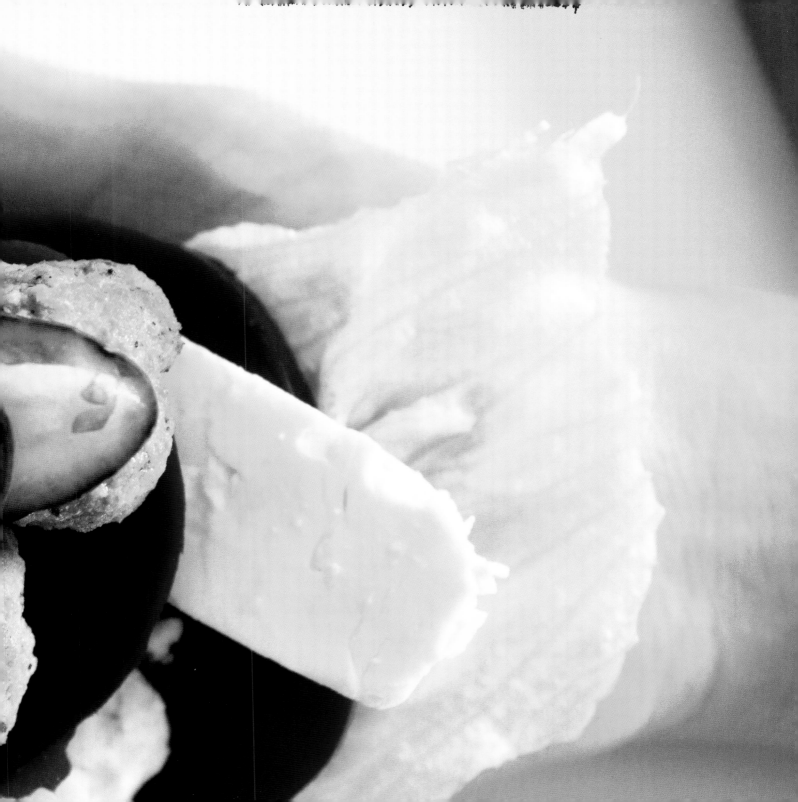

AUTUMN

REINDEER STEW IS OUR INSPIRATION.

INGREDIENTS:

0.5 kg ground elk meat . . . .

0.5 kg ground pork, medium ground . . . .

1 dl breadcrumbs . . . .

1.5 dl regular milk . . . .

2 eggs . . . .

3 juniper and 2 bay leaves, ground with a mortar

DIRECTIONS:

Make the meatballs as you normally would.

Cook up a real autumn stew – in the same pan that you just fried the meatballs in – with chanterelles if available, shallots, butter, 1 dl cream, black pepper and salt, plus a couple tsp lingonberries. Add the meatballs and heat everything together.

Serve with mashed potatoes (which, at this stage, you're an expert at making) and a bowl full of extra lingonberries. Serve vegetables if you so desire.

BEVERAGE TIPS:

For this festive occasion, drink Bad Boy. Don't be intimidated by the name; this is an amazingly well-priced Bordeaux.

WINTER

COLDNESS AND DARKNESS – IS THIS INSPIRATION FOR PAIN OR PLEASURE? WE SAY, DON'T DAMN THE DARKNESS: MAKE A MEATBALL AU GRATIN INSTEAD. OR, MAKE MANY AND STORE THEM IN YOUR FREEZER.

INGREDIENTS:

1 kg ground beef – medium ground . . . .

1 dl breadcrumbs . . . .

1.5 dl whole milk . . . .

2 eggs . . . .

DIRECTIONS:

Make the meatballs as you normally would.

After that, place the balls in the middle of a buttered baking dish with a 3 cm margin on all sides. Pipe the mashed potatoes around them and cover the entire delicacy with:

Cream sauce from the beginning of the book (page 49).

Mountains and mountains of Gruyere cheese, grated as a finishing touch.

Bake at 200 degrees for 15 minutes or until the potatoes and gratin look good enough for Instagram pics.

BEVERAGE TIP:

Depending on your mood and the temperature outside, try drinking Boulard Cidre de Normandie Brut either warm or cold. If you want to warm it up a bit, throw a few apple slices in the pot so that it gives it that extra winter touch. Desire more warmth? Pour a finger or two of Etter Zuger Kirsch – a childhood friend of the cheese.

LUCIA MEATBALLS

DELIGHTFUL YELLOW MEATBALLS THAT ANY SWEDE WOULD BE
PROUD OF DURING THE HOLIDAYS.

INGREDIENTS:

1 kg ground chicken . . . .

1 egg . . . .

1 dl breadcrumbs . . . .

1.5 dl regular milk . . . .

1 package saffron . . . .

0.5 dl finely chopped (don't cheat) raisins . . . . .

Salt and pepper to taste . . . .

DIRECTIONS:

Make the meatballs as you normally would, but wet the saffron in the milk and breadcrumbs before working it into the batter.

BEVERAGE TIPS:

Serve with glögg, which is what the Swedes call mulled wine. If you're feeling cold, warm cider might even be better. Pour 4 dl Brut Domaine de Kervéguen in a pot and warm up to just under 70 degrees. Throw in a few apple slices and dilute with 1 dl of your favorite Calvados. Round out the taste with as much honey as you want and serve piping hot.

CHRISTMAS MEATBALLS

ONCE AGAIN WE'LL USE THE CLASSIC MEATBALL RECIPE.

INGREDIENTS:

1 kg ground beef, medium ground . . . .

1 dl breadcrumbs . . . .

1.5 dl regular milk . . . .

2 eggs . . . .

But with a Christmas touch:

2 pinches cinnamon . . . .

5 allspice and cloves, ground together in

a mortar. . . . .

A fourth of a mug of glögg . . . .

DIRECTIONS:

Prepare in the traditional fashion. For non-bearded chefs, a fake beard (nonflammable and non-criminal looking) worn during cooking can help. But we make no guarantees.

BEVERAGE TIPS:

Can be enjoyed with glögg, a Christmas beer like Sigtuna Christmas Scottish Strong Ale, or Nøgne Ø Underlig Jul, and sparklers.

STEWS

BALL-A-BAISSE

INGREDIENTS:

1 kg ground chicken . . . .

1 egg . . . .

1 dl breadcrumbs . . . .

1.5 dl regular milk . . . .

1 package saffron . . . .

Salt and pepper to taste . . . .

DIRECTIONS:

First, cook the rolled meatballs in chicken bouillon (cubes) for 4-5 minutes. Drain the meatballs and discard the broth.

Now let's get to the stew. Slice in matchstick-size slivers:

1 fennel . . . .

2 carrots . . . .

0.5 celeriac . . . .

1 yellow onion . . . .

3 cloves of garlic (pressed) . . . .

Sauté in rapeseed oil until the ingredients have softened.

ADD:

2 tbsp tomato puree . . . .

0.5 g saffron . . . .

1 can crushed tomatoes . . . .

3 dl water . . . .

0.5 cubes chicken bouillon . . . .

SEASON WITH:

1 star anise . . . .

2 bay leaves . . . .

Salt and pepper . . . .

Let the stew simmer for 15 minutes. Add the meat-balls. Serve as a stew, with aioli and good bread.

AIOLI TIPS:

1 tbsp red wine vinegar . . . .

1 tbsp Dijon mustard . . . .

3 finely chopped garlic cloves . . . .

3 egg whites . . . .

2 dl rapeseed oil . . . .

Whisk the egg whites, mustard, red wine vinegar and garlic together. Add the oil, little by little, at the same time as you whisk. Finish with salt and pepper.

BEVERAGE TIP:

Serve with a Bonterra Chardonnay or a Miraval Rosé Jolie-Pitt & Perrin.

MEATBALLS BOURGIONNE

A WARM STEW FOR COOL EVENINGS.

INGREDIENTS:

150 g diced, smoked side pork . . . .

8 shallots, divided . . . .

100 g mushrooms, cut in quarters . . . .

1 garlic clove . . . .

ADD:

2 tbsp tomato puree . . . .

3 dl Burgundy wine . . . .

2 tbsp Bong's meat bouillon . . . .

2 dl water . . . .

2 bay leaves . . . .

5 sprigs fresh thyme . . . .

DIRECTIONS:

Cook everything together. Brown the meatballs made with the traditional beef recipe. Allow the meatballs to cook together with the stew the last 10 minutes.

Serve with a whole heap of hacked parsley and a freshly baked baguette.

BEVERAGE TIPS:

Goes great with a bottle of Bad Boy.

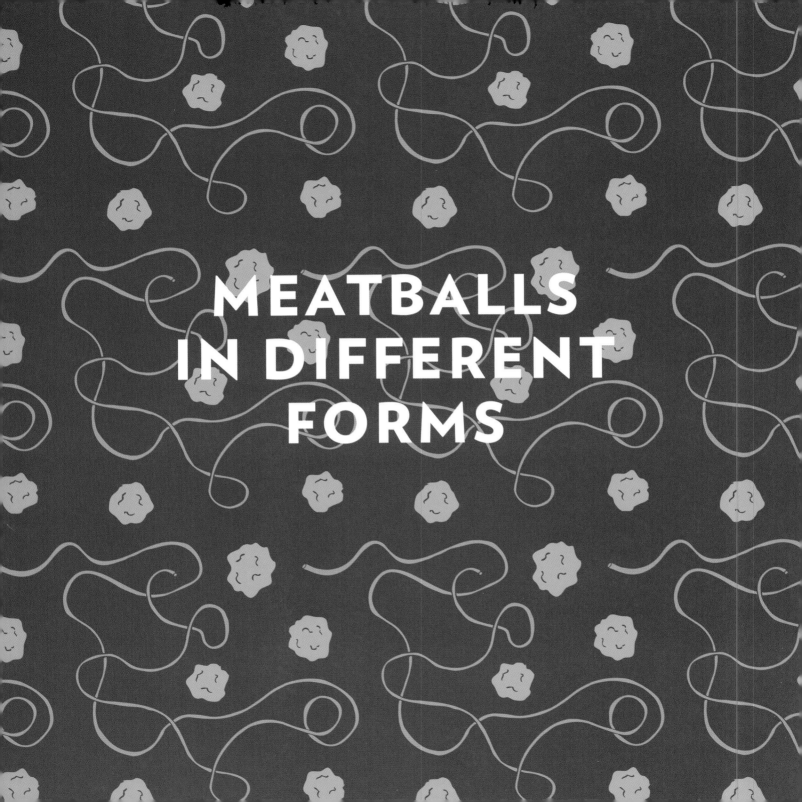

MEATBALLS IN DIFFERENT FORMS

WE WERE AT THE PELICAN. It was the first real meeting of The Swedish Meatball Bible gang, and the mood – after due assessment of the establishment's meatballs (*see kottbullsbloggen.se for a detailed review*) – had reached high levels. Possibly the waiter's eagerness in the beer serving department also had something to do with the creative flow.

"This book should contain unique recipes," we stated. It should feel new, fresh and encourage others to experiment. How do we get that across? By doing the same thing – dreaming up a whole heap of crazy recipes, naturally.

And then the idea came: pickled meatballs.

Pickled meatballs. The fire that immediately lit in Claes's eyes was brighter than a bonfire.

Pickled meatballs are the ideal accompaniment to Christmas, Easter and Midsummer meals. Anyone who doesn't want to eat pickled herring – and we're seeing more and more of them – can get the same flavor (minus the fishiness) with these instead. And what can be a better mix of ancient Swedish traditions than this, we thought? So Claes went home and started on his creation. The recipe, unique to the world, goes a little like this:

PICKLED MEATBALLS

INGREDIENTS:

1 kg ground beef – medium ground . . . .
1 dl breadcrumbs . . . .
1.5 dl regular milk . . . .
2 eggs . . . .
Salt and pepper to taste . . . .

DIRECTIONS:

Use 500 g freshly fried meatballs that have sat and dried on paper towels for a few minutes.

Then combine 1 dl vinegar, 2 cups granulated sugar, 3 dl water, 3 bay leaves and 10 spiced peppercorns. Mix everything together cold until the sugar has dissolved.

Cut 1 carrot and 1 red onion and add to the mixture.

Put the meatballs in a glass jar and pour the mixture over the balls.

Refrigerate for at least 2 days before eating.

This dish goes great with all accessories and drinks that one would traditionally eat and drink when in Sweden at a so-called sill and strömming table (a smorgasbord buffet full of different Swedish fish delicacies).

SEMMEL BALLS

THIS DISH WAS CONCEIVED AS A FUN ADDITION TO ANY MEATBALL BUFFET — AND WE ASSURE YOU IT TASTES AS GOOD AS IT LOOKS.

Start out from the smoked meatballs recipe (see page 130).

Cut off the meatball's "lid" (the top one fifth of the ball). For the filling, we'll use mashed potatoes and a variation of a Waldorf salad, made like this:

INGREDIENTS:

150 celeriac (about half a head) peeled and finely sliced into slivers, then placed in boiling water for 30 seconds before cooling down . . . .
2 apples, core removed, peeled and finely cut into slivers . . . .
2 dl mayonnaise . . . .
1 tbsp walnut oil . . . .
Salt and pepper to taste . . . .

DIRECTIONS:

Dilute with a dash of water if the batter gets too clumpy.

Scoop out meatballs and place in a Waldorf salad. Pipe the mashed potatoes around it, as if it were cream.

We're ready for cocktails!

BEVERAGE TIPS:

Offer your guests a dry cider like Brut Domaine de Kervéguen, an ale like Moinette Blonde BIO and a Pinot Gris Réserve from Alsace. This way, they'll all find their own favorite pairings to go with your Semmel meatballs.

MEATBALL SANDWICH

INGREDIENTS:

1 kg ground beef, medium ground . . . .

1 dl breadcrumbs . . . .

1.5 dl regular milk . . . .

2 eggs . . . .

Salt and pepper to taste . . . .

4 beetroots . . . .

2 egg whites . . . .

1 tbsp Dijon mustard . . . .

1 tbsp white wine vinegar . . . .

2.5 dl neutral cooking oil . . . .

Hönökaka (a Swedish soft bread) . . . .

DIRECTIONS:

Make classic Swedish meatballs using the recipe. Place the meatballs to the side and let them cool.

Boil the beetroots for 20 minutes and then peel. Let cool. Cut the beets in slices and place to the side. Grab the egg whites, Dijon mustard (if available, use Grey Poupon to achieve the intended flavor strength of the recipe), white wine vinegar, and neutral cooking oil. Whisk the egg, mustard and vinegar together in a bowl and add the oil, little by little, as you whisk quickly. Blend the beet slices together with the mayonnaise.

It's never wrong to use hönökaka for bread when serving a classic meatball sandwich. Slather the bread with a thick layer of beetroot mayonnaise. Split the meatballs in halves and situate them atop the mayonnaise in a pleasant pattern. Accompany with a good beer and perhaps even a nice shot of your favorite snaps.

MEATBALL SUB

THIS IS HOW YOU MAKE A REAL "SUBMARINE" AS THE KIDS LIKE TO CALL THEM.

INGREDIENTS:

1 kg ground veal, fresh and finely ground . . . . . .

1 dl breadcrumbs . . . .

1.5 dl cream . . . .

2 eggs . . . .

3 tbsp chopped olives . . . .

3 tbsp chopped sundried tomatoes . . . .

Dressing for each foot long sub:

1 tsp Dijon mustard . . . .

1 tsp honey . . . .

2 tbsp mayonnaise . . . .

1 tsp crème fraiche . . . .

**Real Italian-American tomato
sauce a la nonna:**

2 tsp olive oil (of the highest quality) . . . .

4 finely chopped garlic cloves . . . .

1 finely chopped and de-seeded red chili . . . . . .

1 tbsp finely chopped oregano . . . .

250 g crushed tomatoes . . . .

Salt and pepper . . . .

DIRECTIONS:

Bring to a boil while stirring, then let cool.

Slice open the white submarine bread. Spread dressing generously. Place thinly sliced salami slices atop the layer of dressing.

Cover the salami with sliced meatballs. Flip the sandwich over. Pour tomato sauce over the whole thing.

Cover the tomato sauce with thickly sliced Provolone cheese.

Warm in oven at 200 degrees for 7 minutes or until it starts to look real good.

BEVERAGE TIPS:

Wash down with your choice of sugar free soda or cellar-chilled Brolio in a normal drinking glass.

VIKING MEATBALLS

IF YOU LISTENED TO YOUR HISTORY TEACHER, THE VIKINGS PROBABLY DIDN'T TAKE TIME TO ROLL THEIR OWN MEATBALLS BETWEEN SKULL-CLEAVING CONTESTS, RAIDS, AND ERECTING RUNE STONES. BUT IF THEY HAD, THE TASTE PROBABLY WOULD HAVE BEEN REMINISCENT OF THIS ODE TO VIKINGS, BELOW:

INGREDIENTS:

0.5 kg ground wild boar (if necessary, can be substituted with another meat from the forest such as elk, reindeer, deer, bear or wolf) . . . .

0.5 kg ground pork . . . .

1.5 dl mead . . . .

4 tbsp mortar-ground juniper . . . .

2 tbsp finely chopped Boletus (or any other type of mushroom which grew on the side of the trail on the way home from a hunt) . . . .

4 tbsp blueberries . . . .

1 dl crushed *skorpor* . . . .

Salt and pepper to taste . . . .

DIRECTIONS:

The Vikings were not saints. They did what they felt was natural – but they weren't dumb. So why not let the skorpor (which you delicately part) soak up the mead? Stir from time to time to prevent the porridge from getting clumpy. While the skorpor bread is swelled up fully with the mead, you've already mixed together the other ingredients and planned an invasion of what we now call England. Stir the two batters together, roll the balls, drink mead, ponder compass directions a bit, and then fry what you've got like normal meatballs. Now they're all done. Offer four balls to Frej, the god of fertility and peace, and enjoy a dinner around the hearth.

BEVERAGE TIPS:

What does one drink when eating Viking food? Mead, naturally! Our recommendation is Sommar Mjöd from the district of Kristinehamn in Värmland, Sweden. It's made with honey, chaenomeles, buckthorn and blueberries. Or, try Primator Premium Dark, a dark lager with heavy bitterness that goes well with tasty Viking meatballs.

MEATBALL SANDWICH
À LA PRESLEY

THE LATE KING WAS A SANDWICH EXPERT. OR, BETTER SAID, AN EXPERT IN CALORIC IN-
TAKE. HERE IS A VARIATION OF HIS MOST FAMOUS SANDWICH, KNOWN AS THE "ELVIS,"
WHICH IS GUARANTEED TO GET YOU "ALL SHOOK UP."

FOR EACH SANDWICH:

2 slices white bread (sourdough may be acceptable in certain circles) . . . .

Peanut butter . . . .

Banana slices . . . .

Honey . . . .

Bacon . . . .

DIRECTIONS:

Spread copious amounts of peanut butter on the bread.

Place banana slices on the peanut butter and drizzle a thin layer of honey over it.

Sprinkle finely chopped bacon over the honey. Place the sliced meatballs in a tight layer over the bacon bits.

Heat up a frying pan with butter in it.

Place the sandwich in the pan, brown quickly on one side, turn, and brown the other side quickly.

Grab the sandwich and eat. Wash down with a big glass of Coca-Cola.

Afterwards the world is going to wonder if you're still alive, just as they wonder about Elvis.

BRITISH BULLDOG PIE

RELAX! NO PUPPIES ARE USED IN THE MAKING OF THIS PIE. INSTEAD, WE
TAKE INSPIRATION FROM THE CLASSIC BRITISH STEAK AND KIDNEY PIE,
THE RESULT BEING A MEATBALL VARIATION.

INGREDIENTS:

1 kg ground beef, medium ground . . . .

1 dl breadcrumbs . . . .

1.5 dl regular milk . . . .

PIE DOUGH:

3 dl flour . . . .

75 g butter . . . .

4 tbsp ice cold water . . . .

FILLING:

250 g mushrooms . . . .

2 finely chopped garlic cloves . . . .

3 tbsp finely chopped yellow onion . . . .

2 bay leaves . . . .

1 dl ox bouillon . . . .

1 dl Guinness . . . .

2 tbsp Worcestershire Sauce . . . .

DIRECTIONS:

Cook the filling, covered, for 10 minutes at low heat.

Fry the meatballs as usual.

Work the pie ingredients together into a smooth dough. Put the dough into a medium-sized pie dish with high sides. Save a third of the dough for the piecrust.

Place the meatballs together with the filling in the pie. Add Parmesan, grated generously over everything (bulldogs are famous their love of parmesan cheese!).

Put the piecrust on and bake at 200 degrees on the lowest shelf in the oven for about 30 minutes or until the crust turns a nice color.

BEVERAGE TIPS:

This is a no brainer: Sleepy Bulldog Pale Ale.

ALLIGATOR MEATBALLS

GROUND MEAT:

1 kg ground alligator meat (available at specialist butchers)

INGREDIENTS:

400 g potatoes . . . .

3 tbsp chives . . . .

1.5 yellow onion . . . .

A few bundles of parsley . . . .

3 garlic cloves . . . .

1 celery stalk . . . .

Grind all the ingredients in a meat grinder (as fine a grind as possible) and then add:

2 eggs . . . .

Salt and pepper . . . .

DIRECTIONS:

Roll small meatballs.

Heat the frying oil up, then deep fry the balls until they become golden brown in color and let them dry on a few sheets of paper towel.

Serve with rice and beans.

BEVERAGE TIPS:

When eating alligator meatballs, we like to drink Pabst Blue Ribbon Export and think of Mississippi swamps.

VEGETARIAN MEATBALLS

VOODOO MEATBALLS
(Vegetarian)

INGREDIENTS:

3 black salsify roots . . . .

800 g sweet potato . . . .

4 large beetroots . . . .

DIRECTIONS:

Boil all the ingredients separately. Let everything cool. Grate the sweet potatoes and beetroot. Dice the black salsify.

BLEND IN:

1 egg . . . .

100 g goat cheese . . . .

50 g chopped pecans . . . .

3 tbsp finely chopped chives . . . .

Blend together and fry until desired consistency.

ENJOY WITH:

Black bean sauce

100 g salted black beans . . . .

2 dl vegetable oil . . . .

10 garlic cloves . . . .

2 finely chopped, de-seeded red chilies . . . .

4 cm peeled, fresh ginger . . . .

1 tbsp Chinese black vinegar . . . .

1 tbsp raw sugar . . . .

Heat the oil. Add the garlic, draining the oil when the garlic has some color. Pour the oil back in the pan, add the chili and fry for a few seconds. Remove the chili and add the rest of the other ingredients. Mix well. Let simmer for 3 minutes or until the mixture has scared your black cat out of the kitchen.

BEVERAGE TIPS:

The obvious beer selection is Hell (yes, we know it means "light" in German, but the label is fiery). In actually, a Sancerre Les Belles Dames is probably a better choice – opt for that.

FLOWER QUEENS

(Vegetarian)

INGREDIENTS:

1 kg potatoes . . . .

1 dl chopped herbs (equal parts thyme, basil, rosemary and parsley) . . . .

1 egg . . . .

100 g sheep milk cheese . . . .

Salt and pepper to taste . . . .

DIRECTIONS:

Boil the potatoes. Let cool. Grate with the coarse side of a grater.

Work the ingredients together until they make a nice batter. Roll the balls. Fry in the traditional way in a regular pan.

HUMMUS TIPS:

400 g chickpeas . . . .

2 tbsp rapeseed oil . . . .

1 dl Turkish yogurt (for cooking) . . . .

1 crushed garlic clove . . . .

1 pinch ground cumin . . . .

1 pinch cayenne pepper . . . .

0.5 squeezed lemon . . . .

1 tbsp tahini . . . .

Blend all ingredients in a blender. Enjoy!

BEVERAGE TIPS:

Wash down with organic Reichsrat von Buhl Riesling Trocken.

MEATBALL
ACTIVITIES

MEATBALL ACTIVITIES

NO ONE NEEDS AN EXCUSE TO HAVE A MEAT-BALL FEAST. Properly cooked meatballs are, in and of themselves, a good reason to invite a good group of friends and gather around the dinner table.

Maybe the chef should do it all. On the other hand, it could be pretty cool for party participants to bring their own interpretations and variations on the meatball with them.

A real meatball feast does require several different types of meatballs – like the ones in these pictures, where we tested a number of fun recipes to celebrate the near-completion of our book.

Planning began in the morning. Claes's family had already purchased a number of raw ingredients. All that remained was determining which meatballs were going to be made first. The huge, smoked elk meatballs were ready first, which made it possible for Ralph to put on his oilskin, light up the grill, and defy the winds of spring on the patio. Smoked king-sized meatballs: perhaps the first in the world? We anticipate more of this sort of crazy meatball when The Swedish Meatball Bible starts to circulate.

The rest of the day was a haze of meatball cooking. Large meatballs were intermingled with small ones, based on different ingredients and cooking methods. With a genuine celebrity chef in the kitchen, it really wasn't difficult to bring crazy ideas to life.

At the same time planning was happening on a grand level. Decorating for a meatball feast is a great opportunity to go nuts. A snow lantern made of meatballs –impossible? After a few failed attempts, it stood in all its glory.

A meatball wreath? How about meatball earrings and other stylish accessories? They were no match for clever kids. It all came together spontaneously during the constant, enthusiastic taste-testing of the most recently cooked, elaborately-garnished meatballs.

The table settings for dinner were, unsurprisingly, pretty grandiose. Just about everything that could be there was on the table: liquor, beer, wine and soft drinks abounded as we savored the freshness of spring on the terrace where Ralph, the designated meatball smoker, performed his fiery tasks.

The dinner inspired our photo shoot, and it is the main source of images for this book. "Should we pipe or pour? Place these on the mirror, silver plate or something else? Do we have any vinyl records?"

The composition of dishes should never be underestimated, so why not document it when you're putting it all together? On kottbullsbloggen.se we have a "best-looking meatball meal" competition – come take part!

Eventually, night fell and with it came more guests, eager to try the book's recipes for the first time. We started with light dishes – meatballs with chicken and seafood as a base, and lighter wines – and then gradually increased the weight in both food and drink. The stout, smoked meatballs were met with the appropriate resistance of our powerful Italian wines; and spicier, chili-seasoned meatballs were accompanied by beer. The aroma around the table was made even richer by a meatball lantern, its internal flame possibly keeping its building material warmer than necessary.

Two things turned out to be almost impossible to achieve during dinner: deciding the winning meatball recipe and stopping eating.

MEATBALL CONTEST

WORK ON THIS BOOK REALLY HAD ITS INCEPTION ABOUT 20 YEARS AGO.

For it was then that Hans-Olov and his wife Camilla – in a fit of frustration at not knowing exactly what was included in the prefabricated meatballs that their little one loved above all else – invited a bunch of friends to the first "Renstierna Meatball Open," a competition for honest, homemade meatballs. The competition consisted of two classes: the Classic Meatball and the Custom Meatball.

Classic is of course the traditional meatball's domain, even though there might be different interpretations of what actually makes a traditional meatball.

Custom, however, is the class where everything is possible. In this class, imagination is encouraged and there are no limits – be it form, seasonings or accessories.

All invitees accepted and when the evening competition began there were six dishes in each class to judge.

Most entries came finished, but for the best results some took advantage of the hosts' offer to finish off their dishes in the competition venue's kitchen.

The hosts provided boiled potatoes and other accessories and trimmings, as well as standard drinks such as beer and wine. Some brought their own beverage options, selected specifically to suit their own custom meatballs.

The judging was almost as tough as a state vehicle

inspection even though it was a private affair and took place in several different stages. The traditional meatballs were judged in:

- AESTHETICS AND APPEARANCE
- SIZE
- JUICINESS
- TEXTURE AND COLOR OF THE CENTER
- FLAVOR

... with category scores weighed and merged into one overall score.

For the more imaginative meatballs, there were no fixed criteria: there it was more about creativity, taste, and overall impression.

In fact, several of the meatballs that appear in this book have drawn inspiration from this first competition (among later ones), including the Indian-inspired meatballs, the hunting meatballs and the puff pastry meatballs.

Renstierna Meatball Open has been held several times since; nowadays, the Custom class is typically the only category on the menu. Maybe the competition has even helped to strengthen the modern meatball's DNA and survival?

If you are inspired to hold your own meatball competition, please get in touch with the authors!

MEATBALLS AS AMMUNITION

IN LATE WINTER 2014, I TOOK A DRIVE to a shooting range in one of Stockholm's southern suburbs. A tweed cap sat firmly on my head as my shotgun rested with dignity in its case in the backseat. Earlier in the day I had an interesting conversation with a ballistics expert from one of the major ammunition manufacturers in the Nordic region. I called to discuss the impact energy, exit velocities, powder charges, wind drift and other things that normally are of interest to all ballistics experts. They usually ignite with glee at the first talk of gram weights and powder charges. But there was silence on the line when I asked my question – so much so that I realized he actually took my question seriously.

After some discussions with the manager of the shooting range, I found a secluded corner where I could be alone. I had not told them what I was planning on doing, knowing full well they would think I was a fool. Strangely, I was nervous. Could anything go wrong? Would I endanger myself? Would I damage my gun? Or was I perhaps most nervous at the thought that someone else at the shooting range would discover what I was doing? The truth was probably the latter. With a slightly trembling hand, I set up a clay pigeon on the wooden rack and loaded my gun with a very hard, fully cooked meatball – followed by a shotgun shell.

The ballistics expert on the phone began to ask an unremitting stream of questions. Would the meatball really stay together despite the air pressure? If it split, how could we then calculate the surface area. What powder charge should I use and what pressure curve should we count on? Should the preload be made of felt or plastic? Did I have access to a chronometer to measure the actual speed of the ball?

Then he cleared his throat and asked: "Why? Why are you going to do this?"

I am a little unsure myself why the idea first popped into my head. All meatballs become hard when they are forgotten and not eaten. They are nasty and inedible. But are they useless? Must they be thrown out? How solid can a meatball really be? Might it be possible to use a tough, old meatball as ammunition? Or to go out and shoot clay pigeons with meatballs? Do target shooting with meatballs? I couldn't stop thinking about it and here I stood with a shotgun loaded with a meatball from the Mediterranean family. The meatballs were made specifically by Claes for the shooting experiment. They had been pickled and dried during a comprehensive program. Together we tried to calculate how much the meatballs would reduce in circumference when they dried out so that they would fit perfectly into a 12-caliber rifle. The result was, well, imperfect. I had to push pretty hard with my thumb to chamber the meatball, and the placement of the gunpowder also demanded I push the meatball further down into the cartridge position.

I raised the gun toward the target and took the safety off. It smelled a little like meatballs. And vinegar. I pulled the trigger and suddenly it smelled very much like meatballs and vinegar, and it rained down meatball remnants on the clay pigeon I set up as a target. I fired all the meatballs Claes had made for me to confirm my conclusion. Meatballs are worthless as ammunition.

- RALPH LINDGREN

ACKNOWLEDGEMENTS

RALPH: A big thanks to my family – Lil, Alexandra and Magdalena – and my mother who never served frozen meatballs. To all our friends and colleagues who supported us through all the fun – and sometimes challenging – work on *The Swedish Meatball Bible*.

HANS-OLOV: Thank you Dad, both for all the meatballs and for grandma's handwritten recipes. To Camilla, who always makes food-making fun. And to Selena and Jesper, who will make meatballs for yet another generation to come.

CLAES: I want to thank my mother, Anna Marie, and my late grandmother for all their inspiration and great meatballs.
  And Martina and the kids for all their help and patience.

We also want to give a warm thanks to all the people who participated in our meatball party! Without you this book would never have been half as nice.

Pernilla Berggren
Kajsa Berggren
Axel Berggren
John Eriksson
Hanna Bendes
Lil Larås Lindgren
Alexandra Lindgren
Magdalena Lindgren
Martina Grahn-Möller
Tuva Grahn-Möller
Leo Grahn-Möller
Max Grahn-Möller

The publisher also wants to pass on thanks to Nina Schwab, Katarina Sandart, Sanna Sporrong and Niklas Lindblad for their fantastic work on this book.

/BULLET POINT PUBLISHING
ON BEHALF OF SOFIA EJHEDEN